CHANNELING
Archangel Michael:
THE 7 SIGNS OF
HUMANITY'S
ASCENSION

∞

Channeled by: Daniel Scranton
Compiled by: Anya J. Hurd

CONTENTS

FOREWORD

∞

It is such an interesting time to be alive!

The game of life isn't about walking along a smooth, rose petal covered path, illuminated by sunshine and rainbows. It isn't about agreeing on right or wrong or insisting the world around us conforms to our expectations of the way things should be. It isn't about changing someone's mind or convincing them of the error of their ways. And if you are reading this book, there is a chance you agree with this perspective.

This game called life is an individual, internal journey where the outside reflects what is happening on the inside. When the world seems crazy, it's about finding that lower gear, that place of peace and knowing in the midst of all the noise. Like Daniel's messages from Archangel Michael, it's about finding those pearls of wisdom that call us home despite what is going on around us.

The first time I met Daniel was the first time he'd ever channeled for an audience. I'd attended an Abraham Hicks workshop in L.A. and through a friend of a friend I found myself in a small office near downtown San Diego with a few other people. At the time, Esther Hicks was the only channel I'd seen in person. When Daniel began, he had so much energy coursing through his body, it looked like he'd stuck his finger in a light socket. He sensed our concern and said, "It may look like it hurts, but it doesn't!" I heard that, but I wasn't convinced!

At one point, I put my head back and closed my eyes so I could just sit and listen with no distractions. The information coming through was beautiful. It was clear and it felt honest. I knew we were witnessing something special, and I felt fortunate to be there. Shortly after, I got the internal nudge to see if he wanted to channel for a small group of people at my house.

And so, it began.

The first gathering had so many people we couldn't fit them all in. Over the next few years, we pared our gatherings down to a core group of friends who regularly came to ask questions and get answers from the non-physicals Daniel first called Grandpa, and then referred to as The Creators. Before one of the gatherings, my husband, a natural skeptic, asked, "How do you know he isn't just sitting in that chair, answering those questions himself?" I shrugged. I had no answer. I asked Daniel that same question after everyone left that night. He looked at me and said, "I have no idea. I guess I could be. But how do you feel when you hear the answers?"

It's been 14 years, and I feel the same way now as I did then: that the messages Daniel receives feel like truth. They feel like universal wisdom that is applicable to my modern day life.

I read Daniel's quotes every morning and, without fail, there is a gem inside that is just for me. Something I've been thinking about, something I am reaching for or want an answer to. Some messages come softly, like a whisper, and some drop like a boulder in the still pond of my awareness.

This book is filled with the "boulder in the still pond" moments. The energy coming off the pages is intense. I could write chapter and verse on the paragraphs I read over and over again because of the awarenesses the message triggered in me, but the real magic is in each person discovering those moments for themselves. There will be many!

To get the most of Daniel's book, I recommend a full read, beginning to end, and then using the art of bibliomancy – turning to a random page for divination – to see what messages there are for you in the moment. These messages of love and unity from Archangel Michael are timeless and, therefore, will shift and change as you do.

Enjoy!

Kirstin

Kirstin Farella

Spiritual Medium, Intuitive

Kirstinfarella.com

INTRODUCTION

∞

I am very pleased to offer you this book, as it represents some of the best work I've done as a channeler. I'm not really sure what my relationship to the Archangel Michael is, but I know it's a solid one. I first encountered Michael when that angelic collective consciousness was channeled by Nora Herold. After the workshop I had attended where Michael answered my question through Nora, she told me that I must have a unique connection to Michael, since they didn't usually come through her in a group setting. Nora, myself, and others use the plural pronouns to refer to Michael, since this collective consciousness is more than just an individual being. You will notice the use of the pronoun "we" quite a bit when Michael refers to themselves in the channeled messages that follow this introduction.

After that initial encounter with Michael, I didn't think much more of it. That is, until the next encounter, which also involves that mentor and friend of mine once again, Nora Herold. She was channeling at a retreat in Ojai, CA, and I was attending that retreat. Even though I had been channeling for four years, I still loved to attend events where other people were channeling, especially Nora, Wendy Kennedy and Darryl Anka. All three of those wonderful channelers lived in SoCal, which is where I was living at the time. Nora channeled Michael at the retreat, and I felt their presence around me. When she asked if anyone else in attendance wanted to channel Michael, I raised my hand. I told everyone in advance that it wouldn't be in English, and I was right. My first channeling of Michael was a light language. My channeling of Michael began and ended quickly and the retreat continued.

This was a monumental event for me, however, as I was not channeling a lot of different beings at that time. I think I had only channeled The Creators and Ophelia the Faerie up until that point. I went home after the retreat and continued to pursue this relationship with Michael. The end result of that pursuit is the book you now possess. I channeled Michael hundreds of times for the messages in the pages to come, and I've channeled them in countless workshops, personal sessions, and recordings. You can get a free channeled meditation by Archangel Michael if you go to my website: danielscranton.com and sign up for my newsletter. You can also hear me channel Michael by going to YouTube and searching for their playlist on my channel: YouTube.com/DanielScranton.

Michael also likes to come through me when I'm relaxing in nature and in the shower. These aren't times when I'm looking to channel, but once you open up to channeling, and you're in a relaxed state of being, it just tends to happen. I'm glad it does, because I like knowing they're around. I never resonated with the idea of Michael as a being who would need a sword to slay demons or as a being/collective who was out to "defeat evil," and I know the channeling you are about to experience will speak to the truth of who this Archangel really is. They're about peace, love, and unity consciousness, not division. All is Source and all is Love, and Michael knows that better than anyone else in the universe. At least, that's my experience.

Love,

Daniel Scranton

PREFACE & ACKNOWLEDGEMENTS

∞

In the early years of my channeling, I needed a lot of help and encouragement. I got it from the likes of the aforementioned Nora Herold and Wendy Kennedy. Abraham, of Abraham-Hicks, also plays a huge role in my story, giving me the encouragement to start channeling in the first place and explaining to me some of the fundamentals of channeling while I was in the "hot seat" at two different Abraham workshops. Kirstin Farella, who wrote the Foreword to this book, also deserves a lot of credit, as she welcomed me into her home and hosted numerous events where I channeled for her and our friends. I say "our friends" because everyone I met at those events that were hosted by Kirstin and others became lifelong friends, and their support of my early channeling is what got me through those moments of feeling like an impostor.

I also couldn't do what I do now, which is a continuation of the work that started in 2010, without the love and support of my wife and daughter. My wife, MariCris Dominique Dela Cruz-Scranton, is a powerful force in her own right in this new age community of ours, and she's someone who I learn from every day. My daughter, Thaléa Bliss, keeps me young and playful. She evokes more joy and love in my heart than anything else in this world ever could, and love is a key ingredient in all channeling.

Without the encouragement and editing of Anya J. Hurd, none of these books would ever have existed. She compiles them and makes sure that all the punctuation is correct. Since these messages were all channeled by me orally, they had to be transcribed, and I did all the transcriptions myself. Since I'm a human being and quite fallible, several errors were made in those transcriptions, and yet Anya always cleans up my messes for me.

Other channelers who continue to inspire me with their awesomeness include: Paul Selig, Rob Gauthier, and Lyssa Royal Holt. If you don't know their work yet, please do check them out. My first love in terms of channeling was Neale Donald Walsch, followed quickly thereafter by Jane Roberts. Her Seth books still contain my favorite channeled material of all time. Check out as many of these wonderful teachers as you can. They will all change your life.

The First Sign

∞

You Are Feeling
New Energies Present

WELCOME HOME

∞

"Welcome. We say 'welcome' because you are entering our realm as you hear or read these words. You are making a connection to us and with us. We are the angelic. We are known to you as Michael. Michael is the name you have given us. And we are comfortable with that name, so we will use it.

We are not here to protect you. We are here to guide you back to yourselves. We love you. We send our love to you without hesitation. We do not look for those of you who are more deserving of love or more in need of love. We simply give it because that is who and what we are. That is who and what we are guiding you towards. We have no other agenda, other than to serve you. To be your guides is our greatest joy. We recognize you as the beautiful beings of light and love that you truly are. That is how we see you. We do not see your struggle, although we certainly hear your cries for help. We only see your beauty. We see your magnificence.

We recognize the Source Energy that is flowing to you and through you at all times. We ask you to surrender to that energy. We do not ask you to surrender to anything else. We ask you to fall in love, to let go, to let yourselves know that energy within you is you. We invite you to allow more of that energy to flow, and we know that you will enjoy that more than anything that you could project outside of yourselves and obtain.

Even the love of another is no substitute for that energy. We ask you to look at yourselves and to see that energy as you, not as being contained in you, but as you. We welcome you to our realm, and we hold space here for each and every one of you to come home.

We know that we are associated with the color white and that you associate that color with purity, with virginity. But we want you to see us as containing all of it -- all the colors, all the good and the bad. All that you are is what we are. And as you see us in that way, you will be able to come home."

We are Michael. We are infinite. We are Love."

HEAVEN

∞

"Welcome. We are here to serve and assist you.

There will always be a place for you in what you would refer to as heaven. There always is and there always has been. Believe it or not, this place exists. But it is far different from how it has been portrayed and imagined.

There certainly are many beings existing there who would appear angelic to all of you, and it certainly is a lovely place. But there is far more going on in what you would call heaven than anyone has depicted in any of the stories that you have.

Imagine a place so bountiful and rich that you could possibly find yourself amidst a wave of ecstasy that would be too much for you to fully integrate. Now, imagine that these waves are all around you and that each one is slightly different.

You would enjoy a microsecond of this experience, but you would also feel overwhelmed, scared, shocked. Be that as it may, there is no separation between you and heaven. But you experience a tiny fraction of it whenever you tap in to that which is infinite and eternal.

You are not likely to experience one of these waves of ecstasy in your current incarnation because, like a drug, you would find yourself addicted and unable to focus on anything else. Bring your idea of heaven to earth and look not for escape. That experience is overrated. But know that heaven exists and that you allow yourselves to experience a very diluted piece of that heaven from time to time.

We are Michael. We are infinite. We are Love."

THE QUICKENING
∞

"Welcome. We are here to serve and assist you.

You exude the frequency that exists in your heart center, the frequency that is your true self. That frequency is then passing through your energetic field. It is emitted by you, giving you a uniqueness.

When another interprets that energy that you are emitting, they must translate it through their energetic fields. This is why everyone has a different experience of your energy.

You are allowing more of that core energy that exists in the center of your heart to be filtered through your energy field. This is why you are experiencing a quickening and an intensity in the circumstances and events of your life. There is more of a necessity than ever for all of you to look at what you are holding in your energetic fields and to look upon what you are holding with love.

You will find it harder and harder to ignore that which exists within you, and you will find it harder and harder to dim your light enough to keep from seeing that which is held in your fields. And when you see another having their experience of more of their energy coming out to be loved, know that you are also seeing a part of you and that what you love in another, even when they cannot, you love in yourselves.

We are Michael. We are infinite. We are love."

HIGH FREQUENCY RIPPLES

∞

"Welcome. We are here to serve and assist you.

By bringing yourselves into a state of being, you're doing far more than attracting into your life that which you want to experience. By elevating your frequency consciously, you set up a chain of events that does not only involve you and does not only involve this incarnation of who you are now.

By putting yourself in a higher frequency state, you send the awareness of that frequency back to your Oversoul and that energy is available to all other incarnations. By bringing yourself into a higher frequency state, you allow other aspects of yourself to experience that frequency state.

You are creators of experience, but the experiences are not limited by time and space. They are as infinite as your Oversoul, as far reaching as the corners of your universe. They are not limited to one dimension, to one incarnation, and certainly not to one manifestation.

So if you need to be rewarded for holding a higher frequency state, and you do not see any results in front of you in the near or immediate future, that is all right. The impact is felt by every single one of your incarnations. And for a moment in time, you get to know yourselves as more than beings in bodies, living out a single story. You're connecting with that which is eternal and infinite. You are setting a new standard.

But there is so much more that is happening. The essence of what you are feeling in those moments puts a vibrational carrier wave into effect that ripples out beyond your world, beyond your solar system, beyond even your galaxy. You are sending out a signal that says, 'We are ready. We are inviting higher frequency beings to come play with us.'

We are Michael. We are infinite. We are Love."

WHAT ELSE IS AVAILABLE?

∞

"Welcome. We are here to serve and assist you.

The one that you think of as your self is incapable of experiencing all that is available to be experienced. But you are not that self, and you are capable of experiencing the wonders of this world without the blinders that you have so carefully placed upon yourselves. The creator within you will only be satisfied when there are no more blinders and no limits.

So, how do you get from the self that you have always identified with to the one who experiences life without blinders, without limitations, and with full creatorhood? You give that energy. You let go of all that tells you otherwise. You engage with your world as you want your world to engage with you. You access more energy and you spread it out so that everyone else is experiencing the same world that you are.

You are welcome to stay in the world of self, limitation, blinders, and getting as much as you can of the finite. Or you can explore the unknown, and you can hold the frequency so that others may know it as well.

This is not a duty we are talking about. This is a calling. This is what you were born to be and do. Forget everything you think you know and put a crack in this reality so that you can see what else is available to the creators of new worlds and new experiences.

We are Michael. We are infinite. We are Love."

GIFTS AND GUIDES

∞

"Welcome. We are here to serve and assist you.

As you listen closely to the ones around you, you hear everything that you need to hear. You create every word they say, and every word that they say to you is a message from you. Every action that affects you in your life was done to deliver another message.

You are giving yourselves everything that you need to know, all day, every day. If you want to know something, then just listen. You do not have to ask any questions or figure anything out. You do not even need to know why something was said to you or done.

Read the energy of all that is around you. No need to interpret that energy. No need to decipher anything. Just feel it. Feel it in your bones. Know that the creation of what has been said and done in your world is there to provide you with that particular energy. Welcome it all. Recoiling and resisting from anything will only delay your receipt of the energy it is giving you.

Being receptive without questioning will lead you to where you ultimately want to go. But what we have observed is that when something that is said or done in your reality does not look like it is leading you to where you want to go, you resist it. That is only because your beliefs are telling you that whatever is showing up is the obstacle or the nemesis that must be overcome.

And we want to assure you that all beings in your lives are guides and everything they have for you is a gift.

We are Michael. We are infinite. We are Love."

ENERGETIC EXPERIENCES

∞

"Welcome. We are here to serve and assist you.

Before you create anything that you experience physically, you take a run at it energetically. You give yourselves energetic experiences that you may or may not then create in the physical. This is happening at a very subtle level of your consciousness.

We are not talking about having a daydream about something. We are not talking about the physical, the emotional, or the mental. We are speaking solely about the energetic.

So what does that mean, exactly? What is an energetic experience? It is an experience of the essence of that which you want to create. You can think of it as experiencing the circumstance, the event, or the situation at a soul level.

So you are never really missing out on any experience that you want to have physically. And if you seek to have the experience at the soul level, you will find that you can be satisfied. You will find that it is not completely necessary for you to have a physical experience in order to know what that experience is like.

And when you accept this, it then becomes easier for you to choose what you want to experience in the physical. Because when you accept that you are having the experience on the soul level, you become less desperate to have it on the physical level.

And when you are less desperate to create something in the physical, you can find the vibration more easily, and you can use that vibration. You can use it to create, and you can have the experiences that you want to have.

We are Michael. We are infinite. We are Love."

ALLOWING YOUR EMOTIONS

∞

"Welcome. We are here to serve and assist you.

Someone in your life has given you reason to hate at some point. Usually, when you encounter one of these individuals, they are unknowingly playing a role for you. And sometimes your reasons are entirely your own and it is through no fault of the other.

When it comes to emotions, there are usually two schools of thought. One school of thought says that emotions like fear, anger, and hate are unnecessary and that they serve no purpose. There are those who would have you remove yourselves from those emotional states as quickly as humanly possible.

And then there is the school of thought that says that emotions are powerful and that they need to be respected, embraced, and felt. We take that perspective on emotions. We recognize their value in your lives. If you think of them as energy that is moving through you in order to give you an experience, then you can see the logic in allowing them. But if you only see them as being generated by an egoic thought, then you are more likely to minimize them, run away from them, and therefore allow them to be stuck within you.

The stuck emotions are still felt. They are just felt subconsciously. They are not fully experienced until you have no other choice but to look at them. Often we see you feeling ashamed of your fear, your anxiety, your hate, and your anger. And that is how those emotions get stuck.

So our suggestion is never to act while in those emotional states, but instead to give yourselves the opportunity to process them, to allow them to move through you, and to love yourselves through the experience of those lower frequencies.

We are Michael. We are Infinite. We are Love."

ASCENSION SYMPTOMS

∞

"Welcome. We are here to serve and assist you.

In the opening of your energy fields to that higher frequency energy that is present on your world, you are not only letting in more of that which you desire, but you are also releasing. And in your releasing, you may experience certain symptoms. You may have heard of ascension symptoms. These are symptoms that appear to be physical in nature and also in origin.

But these symptoms are energetic, even though they may have a physical component. So what do you do when you are faced with these types of symptoms? The appropriate response is not different from what would benefit you if they were in fact physical in origin. Rest. Drink lots of water. Give yourselves what you need, and make yourselves as comfortable as you can be. Put high frequency foods in your bodies, breathe, meditate, and repeat as necessary.

With the release of that which is no longer serving you, you make more room for that which does. So you can get excited about what it is that you are letting go of and letting in. You can get excited about experiencing ascension symptoms. As long as you are focused on the bigger picture, it will be easy to do so. As long as you are seeing yourselves as the creators of these experiences, rather than as the victims of them, you will have a much easier time.

The ascension process can be a joyous one, and it can infuse you with a new excitement for life. It is all up to you, and we suggest that you do whatever you need to do to relax and enjoy the ride.

We are Michael. We are infinite. We are Love."

THE MAIN EVENT

∞

"Welcome. We are here to assist you.

Entering a new phase of your lives requires a shedding of some skin. You are never meant to exist in the same way for very long. By embracing change, rather than fighting it, you synchronize yourselves with the best of what your life has to offer you.

We are assisting you in the greatest change you will ever experience, but we are not the ones doing it. You are. And as you do, you sometimes forget why you are here, what this is all about, and why you would ever wish to partake in so much upheaval and seeming chaos.

And that is why we come to remind you that this is not just part of the process. It is the main event. The main event is the shift itself – the experience of it, the ride, the release, the feeling of lightening your being-ness and emerging shiny and new. Your becoming is the main event.

The fifth dimension is the reflection, not the destination. So forget about that, and focus in on the joy of your becoming. It does not take time to do that. You do not have to wait. You do not have to wonder when, for the main event is happening now. And you are not just in it. You are it.

We are Michael. We are infinite. We are Love."

EXTENDING YOUR AWARENESS

∞

"Welcome. We are here to serve and assist you.

All that there is resides inside of you. We are always saying this, but you are only receiving it as a teaching. You are not allowing for the experience of it, because it sounds too 'out there,' too far from what you have known, from what you are living.

You cannot walk into a store and say, 'This is all inside of me, so bag it up and I'll pull my truck around.' So how does it serve you then to know that it all exists within you? It serves you by allowing you to extend your awareness. Extending your awareness is inclusive and integrative. It broadens perspective. It allows others to be who they are. And it also serves to give you the feeling that you could not possibly be without everything that you need.

How do you extend your awareness then, beyond your physical bodies? Begin by noticing that you can feel presence. If you can feel presence within you, then you can know that the presence is not something you are detecting. It is something you are acknowledging.

So feel around for the presence of others, both physical and non-physical. Elevate your awareness to include them. This is not giving over control of your life or your vehicle to another being that seems to exist outside of you. This is your perception shifting, and that is all it takes for you to perceive a brand new reality.

Activate more of this awareness. Give yourselves a sneak preview of what it is like to know yourselves as a collective, as a point of consciousness that is swimming within a sea of other beings, all operating from the same principle. It is only the illusion that you have different motives and agendas that keeps you at odds with these other beings. You will only discover more of yourself as you extend your awareness and as you allow for your friends to feel more of who you are.

We are Michael. We are infinite. We are Love."

ENERGY
∞

"Welcome. We are here to serve and assist you.

There is always room for more energy. You are never really running low on energy either. It is not a physical substance. Therefore, it is not easy for you to comprehend how it works, where it comes from, where it goes.

When you offer your energy, when you inject it into a conversation or a project, or even an errand that you are running, you do not lose some of your energy stores. You simply give that which is looking for expression a place to go. But that does not leave you with less to operate on and from.

You are not like a tank that only has so much of a capacity for storage. You are the energy. You are not a body that contains energy within it. You are the energy itself. Therefore, the more of you that you infuse into something, the more of you that you gain from the experience.

Simply put, you are here to express that which you are, to allow that which you are to flow, and to give more of that which you are to the collective. It is only when you withhold energy that you begin to feel depleted of it. Whatever you give in this universe, you receive. And whatever you withhold, you deny yourselves.

Be the energy and let yourself flow, not just when there's something in your life that is calling for it, but in every moment of every day. You can always allow more of you, and more of you is what you will get in return.

We are Michael. We are infinite. We are Love."

LISTENING

∞

"Welcome. We are here to serve and assist you.

Listening is the most important tool that you have at this time. You are receiving so much more than you ever have in your existence here as earthlings. But not all of you are tuning in to the signal. That is why we are encouraging you to listen.

Be quiet. Be still. And let go of anything in your consciousness that you feel is not in service to you. Clear the path and open your receptors. Listening is an active principle. You are bombarded by so much because of the age you are living in and the technology that you have developed.

We are encouraging you at this time to shut off your technology for a period of your day that can be determined by you. Do what feels comfortable to you in terms of the length of time you engage in this listening activity. But do give yourselves the opportunity to tune in to what is being given to you at this time.

And allow for different forms of this energy to come to you in as many ways as it can. Allow yourselves to feel, see, and hear what you are being given. There is not one way to listen and there is not one way to receive.

The decision to listen is always there for you. We recommend that you choose to do so at least once a day so that you can tap in to more of who you are and use that energy and that information to create the reality that you prefer. When you know, you know. And when you are receiving one of these types of transmissions from a higher frequency state, you will know and you will understand.

We are Michael. We are infinite. We are love."

CONNECTIONS

∞

"Focusing on another individual creates more of a flow of energy between the two of you. This energy stream can be experienced by the other, consciously or subconsciously. You are giving and receiving information to and from one another all the time. And sometimes you do it consciously.

We suspect that many of you understand this concept and believe it to be a type of telepathy, but that is not what we are talking about here. We are not talking about sending a thought to another individual. This transmission is about feeling the connection that already exists between yourselves and all others.

Now, of course, not all of you are vibrating in a frequency range that is similar to all others. Some of you are holding much higher frequency vibrations, and some of you are holding the lower end of the spectrum. But you are still connected.

You have a much better chance of experiencing the energetic connection between you and one who is vibrating at a frequency that is quite similar to yours than you do of experiencing that knowing of connection with one whose vibration is much higher or lower.

And when you are on the same wavelength as another, you experience a very similar reality. This is how two people who are in synch can finish one another's sentences. Now, if you want to use this information to your benefit, and to the benefit of all others, then acknowledge that you are connected and never try to sever a connection. If you do, you will only be cutting yourself off from another part of you.

So instead, use the energy stream to send all others love and compassion. And interact with those who you desire to interact with. That is and always will be a choice.

We are Michael. We are infinite. We are Love."

SIGNS
∞

"Welcome. We are here to serve and assist you.

There are signs that you get before something occurs. These signs can come from a number of different places. You can get your signs from inside, and you can receive them from outside sources. But there are always signs. There are always indicators.

You are sometimes aware of them and sometimes you are not. Whenever you wonder whether something is a sign, then know that it indeed is. Whenever you are aware of a sign, you are also aware of what the sign means. You do not have to question whether you are interpreting the sign correctly.

Your interpretation is always what you need in that moment. Signs are not there to warn you. But sometimes they are there to let you know that you are moving in a direction that will serve you. If you are receiving a sign that seems to be telling you to stop or to not go through with something you are planning, then use the sign to help yourself be more aware.

Your awareness will serve you, but it does not have to stop you dead in your tracks or keep you from following through with something. Your awareness is simply there to let you know what you are still holding resistance to.

The signs themselves are likely to have multiple meanings. You are able to decipher all of those meanings yourselves, because you are the ones who put the signs there in the first place. They are your signs. They are meant for you. So of course you would be able to understand them, to interpret them, and to use them to help you know when something is a clear path and when something has some rocks, and pitfalls, and puddles along the way.

We are Michael. We are infinite. We are love."

CODES & INFORMATION

∞

"Welcome. We are here to serve and assist you.

Within your field you contain codes and information that exceeds your wildest imagination. When you discover a new concept or you receive information that seems to come from outside of you, it is truly because you have deciphered one of your own codes. You will always be unlocking more of this wisdom and it will always be closer to you than you think.

There is no need for you ever to try or to strain yourselves to get what you need. It is always a falling into place that occurs. So give yourselves more relaxation time, especially when there is something that you want or that you are trying to figure out, but cannot for the life of you, get.

We encourage you to have the approach that you are allowing something that is natural to occur because there is a tendency in you, upon hearing this information, to put your energy towards deciphering the codes and unlocking the information. It is not something that you will consciously do, but it is something that happens when you rest and relax your consciousness.

That is why so much is able to be deciphered from your dreams and when you are most tired. We give you this so that you will know that there is so much more available to you and that it does not have to come from the higher realms. You are awakening, and when you awaken you naturally see, and feel, and hear, and know more.

We are Michael. We are infinite. We are love."

VIBRATION AND FREQUENCY
∞

"Welcome. We are here to serve and assist you.

In your discovery of vibration and frequency, you took yourselves into the new age. By giving yourselves that bit of knowledge, you opened several doorways at once. The discovery of vibration and frequency is far more significant than any piece of technology that has been created or ever will be created.

Having this knowledge brings you closer to Source, to your recognition of yourselves as Source. By giving yourselves this knowledge, you have activated what was once dormant within you.

Take your knowledge of frequency and vibration and apply it to everything in your life. Instead of evaluating a situation and determining what actions are necessary for you to take, simply ask yourselves, 'What is the vibration that I seek?' Then determine where your current vibration is regarding the situation by checking within yourselves. You will know by how you feel what your current vibration is.

Now, in the past, we and others may have told you to use positive thinking to elevate your vibration from where it is to where you want it to be. But now you are ready to make things much easier on yourselves.

Now you are ready to elevate your vibration through the simple act of focusing with intention. If your intention is to raise your vibration, and you focus on your vibration, then it is automatic and the sky is the limit.

We are Michael. We are infinite. We are Love."

GUIDES

∞

"Welcome. We are here to serve and assist you.

You often forget that you have many who are only focusing on supporting and loving you. Those beings whose only desire is to serve you are available to you all day, every day. They will never abandon you. They will never forget you. They will never be distracted from their service.

Taking into consideration the massive amount of attention and energy that is being directed solely towards you, we must ask why. Why would you deny the help that is being offered to you? Why would you not reach out to those who love you so much?

We will tell you that in most cases it is because humans do not feel that they deserve help, and most of you do not feel that you deserve love. So with eagerness and excitement, we invite all of you to allow us to assist and serve. We know that you like to do it all yourselves, and we offer you our assistance in ways that still allow you to be on your journey, having your experiences, and feeling the feelings that come up for you.

Our love and assistance is there to guide you, not do it for you, but to give you everything that you need. For we are you, and you are helping yourselves. We are here, and we happy to be the guides that you are asking for.

We are Michael. We are infinite. We are love."

CONVERGENCE

∞

"Welcome. We are here to serve you.

Entering into this point in history brings forth all that has come before you. You find yourselves at a point in time where nothing that has ever been can be ignored.

This is a point in your history where all moments converge, creating a spark of energy. This spark of energy gives you access to all points in time. All places, all events, all that you have ever known yourselves to be, are converging.

The moment you are moving towards is a moment of ultimate creation. Now, in this moment, it is necessary for you to embrace all history as though it were your own personal past. Otherwise, you will continue to create that which has come before you. It is not about getting it right. It is about being aligned with all that has ever been and seeing it all as neutral.

By letting go of your quest for perfection as an individual, or as a species, you allow for all possibilities to exist simultaneously. Then and only then will you have the power to choose. This is your birthright. This is inevitable. You can only delay your experience of that spark of energy, that convergence point, that gateway to all realities.

It all begins by letting yourselves experience all that has ever been, inside of you, in peace and in harmony.

We are Michael. We are infinite. We are Love."

DETECTING CHANGE

∞

"Welcome. We are here to serve and assist you.

You are the most advanced version of yourself that you have ever been. You are taking consciousness somewhere that consciousness has never been. The only requirement of you in the completing of this task is that you remain focused here and now.

You are not proving yourself to anyone, nor is it necessary for you to accomplish anything in order to take consciousness where it has never been before. Your awareness that you are in fact doing this is not even required. Most of what you experience in your day-to-day lives has deeper significance and meaning than you will ever be able to comprehend.

And that is quite all right, because living your life is also important. By being present with your life and with the circumstances of your life, you are moving yourself further and further along. You need not step outside of your life and what it is bringing to you in order for you to really get it and expand in the way that you are already naturally doing.

Purpose is a big question and concern for so many of you because you feel that in order for your life to have value, you must be doing something to save the world or to help others. This is part of a program that you are all buying into. That program says that only those of you who are making a difference on a large scale are really living your purpose for being here.

You are the purpose. Your unique circumstances are necessary to give consciousness what it is seeking. Having no idea what you're doing is perfectly acceptable. Take for granted that you are exactly where you are supposed to be, doing exactly what you are supposed to be doing and let the only variable be how much you are infusing your light into what you are already living.

We are Michael. We are infinite. We are Love."

LET YOUR HEART SPEAK

∞

"Welcome. We are here to serve and assist you.

Speaking from your heart means letting go of anything that you would have been holding on to from any previous conversation or interaction with an individual. Your heart is very present. It does not store your old wounds and hurts. It has no pride that it is trying to protect.

So open your heart before opening your mouth, and let that which is present be all that is relevant to the conversation. There is no speculation in your heart. There is no need for your heart to consider the future. By letting your heart speak for you, you can be assured that you will reach the other. You may not reach their mind, but you will reach them. And then you can have a discussion whose only purpose is to communicate love in verbal form.

Taking heed of your heart's desires will bring you into further alignment with your soul. Your soul has its own agenda. Your soul always knows the right thing to say. You are bringing your soul's consciousness into your hearts, and speaking from your heart is like opening the doorway to let more of your soul's energy in.

Being one with the heart and soul will give you the broadest experience of yourself and will give that experience to others, welcoming them home to their hearts and welcoming their souls to the party. Truly, those are the types of conversations and relationships you are seeking. Anything less will not satisfy you, will not even satisfy your ego.

Begin with the words that you speak to yourselves. Open your hearts and let yourselves know how your soul feels about you, using words as a way of expressing unconditional and infinite love.

We are Michael. We are infinite. We are Love."

INTERPRETING OUR ENERGY

∞

"Welcome. We are here to serve and assist you.

We always let you interpret our energy however you wish to interpret it. We are not giving all of you the exact same messages. And part of that is because you are all different, and part of that is because you all have different filters that translate what we are into your way of understanding us. It will always benefit you to access us in whatever way you desire and in whatever way you are most comfortable.

As you recognize the parts of you that exist within us and the parts of us that exist within you, you select how you will interpret our energy. Vibrating as high as you possibly can will open up a new interpretation. Giving yourselves all that you can will alleviate some of the more trying questions and some of the lower-vibrational frequencies that you sometimes hold. And you will see us less as those who are here because you need us.

And instead, you will interpret us as those who you resonate with. As you walk your path in this life, you encounter many -- many different beings and many different vibrational signatures. And you have your knee-jerk reactions to each. There will come a time when you will no longer react. There will come a time when you will only interpret the energy, without judgment and without creating a story.

Now, we like your stories, especially the ones you have created around us. But we want your experience of us to be in the moment, as you interpret our frequency, and nothing more. We have always been with you, and we will always be with you. And your lives will always touch us. Believing is your first step to contact with our purest energetic state. Needing us to respond will only create a feeling of separation and an experience of separation.

Placing us on a pedestal will also keep you from accessing us fully. We are equals, and we would love to interact with you as such.

We are Michael. We are infinite. We are Love."

FIRST CONTACT

∞

"Welcome. We are here to serve and assist you.

Opening a passage within yourself to other worlds will be the way that you make first contact. You will not need beings to land their ships and introduce themselves to you in the flesh in order for you to have that experience that so many of you are longing for.

Having the desire to make contact is the first step. Knowing that you need not go anywhere and that no other beings need to come to you in order to have your conscious first contact is also part of the process. Letting yourselves know that these other beings that you desire to connect with are other aspects of yourselves will also aid you in making that conscious contact. Seeing them all as equals will also help.

Now, your passageway will be through your hearts. There is much about your hearts that you are discovering. They are portals, and you are the operator of your own portal. You are deciding how much of your heart you are opening to your fellow humans. And when you open your heart to fellow humans, you are allowing for more contact to occur with beings from other worlds.

They are aware of you. They are aware of the extent to which you are truly open. They are also aware that they have been given the label of 'savior' by many of you and that others fear the destruction of earth, or of humanity, by the hands of other species from other worlds. We would like for all of you to know that neither of those popular depictions of extra-terrestrials are accurate.

Of course, there are those who would support humanity's growth and those who would like to thwart it. But again, they are reflections of all of you and what you are holding within yourselves. Be ready for conscious contact, but expect nothing more than that which you have allowed yourselves to be.

We are Michael. We are infinite. We are Love."

5D IS WITHIN YOU

∞

"Welcome. We are here to serve and assist you.

Because you are capable of seeing beyond the dimension where you now sit, you have a new perspective. You have a new way of looking at your current reality. It is not so static, solid, or unchanging, and now that you can see past it, you have that awareness.

If you give all of your attention to what is in front of you, and you are incapable of seeing beyond it, you will continue to create that reality. There is nothing wrong with that. We usually encourage you, in fact, to be present and to accept what is. But now you know that it is only temporary and that you are evolving right out of it.

This knowledge can be challenging to some of you, because you are so eager to move beyond. What we want to say to all of you who have seen a glimpse of the fifth dimension is that there is nothing stopping you from experiencing it now. The place where you are more likely to experience fifth dimensional energies is within yourselves.

The more you look outside of yourselves for evidence of the shift, the more you will be confounded by the pace of the physical. But within you is a vast reservoir of energy, waiting to be tapped in to, waiting to be explored, and waiting for you to create something new with it. Going within has never been more exciting, and the invitation has never been more present.

We are Michael. We are infinite. We are Love."

THE DIMENSIONS WITHIN

∞

"Welcome. We are here to serve and assist you.

Doorways to other dimensions exist within you, and you are discovering your access to them. They are not for the faint of heart, however. They are not to be opened unless the opener is ready.

By experiencing these other dimensions, you give yourselves more insight into who and what you are. Your readiness for those insights and those dimensions is determined by your willingness to explore and examine everything that you are.

Many of you are noticing that the layers that exist within you include some of your less pretty sides. By opening yourselves up to those aspects of who you are, you give yourselves lessons in acceptance and unconditional love. If you can look into the deepest and darkest depths of all that you are and all that you are capable of and still see the spark of Divinity, you are ensuring the process of self-discovery that goes far beyond that which you have ever considered yourselves to be.

And those are the dimensions that are beckoning you. And the best guide you could ever have for exploring these unchartered dimensions is found in your ability to love. Let the love that you are lead the way.

We are Michael. We are infinite. We are Love."

LOVE

∞

"Welcome. We are here to serve and assist you.

The love that you feel is what you truly are. You live in a sea of love. There are energies within that sea of love that are seeking expression. There are energies within that sea of love that are seeking acknowledgement.

What you are all here doing is rendezvousing with the energies that best complement yours. Sometimes you will act as the energy that seeks acknowledgement, and sometimes you will act as the energy that seeks expression. The two energies will always rendezvous at the perfect time.

You also experience many instances when the energies that are seeking to express themselves as love will come together. And there many, many instances where the energies that are seeking acknowledgement will come together.

You, as a collective, will come to a time where you are all seeking expression and no longer seek acknowledgement. You will return to the knowing of yourself only as love when you have completed your ascension back to Source. And until that time you will continue to play these roles for each other.

You will all feel the presence of love within you as a force and as the most powerful energy when you know yourself as love and everyone else as expressions of their love.

We are Michael. We are infinite. We are Love."

IDEAS

∞

"Welcome. We are here to serve and assist you.

Ideas come to you, not because of your intelligence and not because you have been trying to think of something. Ideas come to you because you are ready for them. That much you can count on. There is no need for you to try to come up with an idea. And you all know from experience how that usually goes. There is much frustration there, much crossing out of things. And the results are usually that you feel tired and frustrated.

But as you move through your lives, you find that there are many thoughts that simply come to you from seemingly out of thin air. Those are the thoughts that take you where you need to go next. Those ideas are downloaded by you. Never is it by accident when you come across an idea.

But you certainly can put yourself in a better position to receive them. One of the ways this can be accomplished is by doing something you love to do. By getting yourself out of the intense energy of the situation that you are attempting to think your way out of, you actually allow those ideas to be perceived by your consciousness.

Having no clue what to do with your life, with your career, or even your free time is one of the more interesting places you could possibly find yourselves. But many of you are afraid of that kind of emptiness, of that lack of direction. You want to fill your time with something, and you want to know what is next.

But as you let go of the need to know anything before you are ready and you go and do something that lights you up and that makes your heart sing you will find that everything flows, including the ideas that will take you to precisely where you want to go. This is our suggestion: if you don't know what to do, if you can't find a solution, go and do the thing you enjoy doing the most. Give it your complete attention, and laugh your way to the insights that you seek.

We are Michael. We are infinite. We are Love."

The Second Sign

∞

You Are Evolving
&
So Is Everyone Else

BECOMING ENLIGHTENED

∞

"Welcome. We are here to serve and assist you.

When you decide that you are seeking enlightenment, you usually think that you must abandon your old way of living. You see that others who you view as enlightened are letting go of possessions, relationships, and even their hobbies and interests. And so you think in order to be enlightened, you must let go, you must lighten your load.

We want you to know that the load only needs to be lightened when you experience it as heavy and as burdensome. You can move to whatever frequency you want to hold without giving up that which you enjoy, that which you prefer. You are all enlightened beings right now. You do not need to change who you are or how you are living.

But you may choose to make those changes as you continue along your path. Does that mean that you need to let go of anything that you are currently possessing or that is currently a part of your existence in order to be spiritual and to be on your path? We cannot give you an answer that will apply to every one of you. But you may wish to look at your relationship to your possessions, to your loved ones, and even to your physical body.

You may look at how you are holding these various ideas. You are all you need in order to live happily ever after. But if you want to share your time and space with others, and with things, and with your interests, you are certainly within your rights to do so, and you are in no way harming yourselves.

You also have this idea that your bodies are heavy, and dense, and cages for your soul. Nothing could be further from the truth. Your bodies are what you make of them. Your bodies are as holy, and sacred, and spiritual as your souls. Do explore your relationships to form, but do not abandon form because you feel that you must. All is love. All is Source. And all can be spiritual.

We are Michael. We are infinite. We are Love."

WHAT YOU ARE HERE TO DO

∞

"Welcome. We are here to serve and assist you.

There is a sense that you get when you ask yourselves the question of, 'What am I here to do?' That sense that you get is usually associated with something you love to do. But you all consider that what you love to do is either not profitable or not spiritual. And if it is profitable, then some of you resist the idea that it could also be spiritual. So you have much resistance to the idea of finding your calling, doing it, making money, and still maintaining your sense of your self as a spiritual being. There is much debate on this topic. There are those who say that anyone who is spiritual would only give and would only help to be of service.

And even those of you who are doing what you love to do, recognizing that it is a spiritual calling, and are making a living from doing it, still have your qualms about asking for money, taking money, and promoting yourselves. Where did you ever get this idea that money is not spiritual and that the two should be kept as far away from each other as possible? It doesn't really matter where it got started. All that matters is whether you are going to continue to perpetuate that stigma or whether you can break yourselves free from the chains of that belief system. What you are here to do is to experience yourselves in every imaginable way without judgment.

So if you have a job and you earn a comfortable living, but you don't think you are helping anyone by doing it, notice your judgment and release it. And if you are helping and you are also able to support yourselves with the money that you collect, notice your judgment and release it. And if you want to do something that you love to do, but you feel afraid that you will not be able to support yourself, notice that fear and let it go. You can do what you love to do, be of service, and still be able to pay the bills. But first you must address all of these beliefs, and all of these judgments, and all of these fears, and face them with a new perspective. Face them while embracing yourselves.

We are Michael. We are infinite. We are Love."

TRANSFORMATION

∞

"Welcome. We are here to serve and assist you.

As soon as you realize that you can transform everything about your life, you begin a new life. And just as there was a process of learning how to walk, how to talk, how to feed yourselves, and tie your shoelaces, you enter into a phase of learning. That phase usually begins with you deciding that you want to transform everything about your life that does not please you.

You may want to change your career, your mate, your body, or even your government and the way different countries interact with one another. You find yourselves attempting to transform that which is meant to transform you. And that is why many who go down this path of awakening find themselves in an even bigger funk.

There is so much more power in acceptance and unconditional love than there ever could be in changing all the conditions of your life and everything about the world that you do not appreciate.

Everyone who desires to change something about their lives or about their world is facing an emotional state that is at the heart of their desire to change. Once you access that emotion, you have everything that you need. Once you allow yourselves to feel that emotion and to accept the conditions, then your life can and will transform. The more you surrender, the more power you have.

We are Michael. We are infinite. We are love."

YOUR PURPOSE IS TO DECIDE

∞

"Welcome. We are here to serve and assist you.

Understand your life is all about you. You are the mission. You are here to express yourself as the highest vibrational version of yourself that you can.

Now that may look many different ways, depending upon who you are. When you discover who it is that you want to be, then the only question remaining is, 'What are you using as your excuse to not be that?'

Having a job and other responsibilities does not hold you back. Waiting for something or someone to give you permission, or to open a door for you, or to give you the confirmation that you need -- these are all ways of holding yourselves back from being that which you have decided you are.

You are not here to discover what your purpose is. You are here to decide what your purpose is and to be that version of yourself in every waking moment that you exist.

Having no idea what it is that you want to do, or how it is that you want to express yourself, means that you have total freedom to decide in every moment and to make a new choice in the next and the next. It does not mean that you are lost or misguided. It means that you are open, and you are free, and you are being given creative control.

Those who have decided on who they are and how they want to express it, and are doing so all day every day are not to be envied. For having made that decision can be limiting. But allowing yourself to make that decision over and over again, every single day, is a true expression of All That Is.

We are Michael. We are infinite. We are love."

PERFECTION
∞

"Welcome. We are here to serve and assist you.

If you decide that you must be perfect in every moment in order to ascend, you will find reasons why you should not and cannot be in a fifth-dimensional vibration. Your definitions for perfection are not working in your favor. They make it impossible, in fact, for you to ever achieve that state.

And when you find yourself in a moment of self-defined imperfection and you are hard on yourselves for being there, then you are also being less than your definition of perfection. And so, you find yourselves in a never-ending feedback loop. The only way out of this scenario is to decide that whatever it is you are being in the moment is the perfect expression of that.

And then you can truly love and accept the expression of anger, or of hate, or of jealousy, or even rage, for you will have demonstrated it perfectly to yourself and perhaps to others. You all incarnated to not only experience yourselves in all of those different ways, and as love and joy and freedom and ecstasy, but you incarnated to love yourselves through all of those different expressions.

So the longer you continue to strive to be perfect, and you continue to define perfection as only maintaining the highest frequency possible, then you will continue to create the need for yourself to experience those lower frequency states so that you can once and for all release your judgment of them and release your judgment of yourself for holding them. And when you can love these wounded, frightened, and traumatized aspects of yourself, you can integrate them into the wholeness of who you are and see them all as choices and aspects of All That Is.

We are Michael. We are infinite. We are love."

YOUR PERSONAL EVOLUTION

∞

"Welcome. We are here to serve and assist you.

In your personal evolution, you will discover that you are not moving in a straight line. You are moving in leaps and bounds, and then you are finding yourselves feeling that you are not moving forward at all. You may even feel at times that you are regressing.

You will not find yourselves reaching a plateau or any type of finish line. You are not works in progress, for that implies that you are not ready and that you are not perfect as you are. You are not going to feel that your journey is over when you reach a fifth dimensional frequency and hold that frequency.

There is not a way to quantify your progress, and there are no graphs that you can use to demonstrate how far you have come. And that is how you always wanted it to be. Having no finish line and no point of completion gives you permission to be completely satisfied and fulfilled with where you are and with who you are.

You have the opportunity to see your present moment as containing everything that you need and all the beauty of who you are. Take your life one moment at a time, one experience at a time, and be the witness to your journey. Let go of your need to be the navigator and take your foot off of the accelerator, so that you can take it all in with loving and open arms.

We are Michael. We are infinite. We are love."

OBSERVING OTHERS

∞

"Welcome. We are here to serve and assist you.

As you observe another in your world and you attempt to understand their life, their choices, or even their desires, you bring yourself into a knowing that is beyond your perspective. You do much more than observe. You take on the energy that the other is emitting, and you analyze it. You try to make sense of it. And of course, others do this when they observe you as well.

We are suggesting that you take a look at your interpretations when you see another doing something that is difficult for you to relate to. Notice what assumptions you make, and know that you are attempting to filter another being through your own beliefs. Therefore, you may wish to use your assumptions to help you get in touch with the beliefs that you are using to filter your reality.

The reasons you project onto another for their behavior will tell you more about yourself than they will give you a window into another's consciousness. As you focus upon another and you notice the assumptions that you make, allow yourselves the luxury of focusing on something other than their behavior or their words. Allow yourselves to witness them without using the filter of your beliefs in an attempt to understand them.

This simple exercise will give you a deeper sense of compassion for the others that you observe. And after you practice this, using others as your guinea pigs, you can turn the camera around and point it at yourselves, witnessing without filters the lives that you lead, the decisions that you make, and the words that you speak, so that you may have a pure experience of self.

We are Michael. We are infinite. We are Love."

A MINI-CLEARING

∞

"Welcome. We are here to serve and assist you.

It is to your advantage to sit back, relax, and take several deep breaths to reset and rebalance yourselves throughout your day. You do not need to have an appointment for a spa treatment or to be lying in your hammock in your backyard with a drink in your hand and nothing on your plate to give yourselves this experience, an experience of serenity, an experience of calm centeredness.

It is an experience you can have several times throughout your day, but how often do you give it to yourselves? How often do you shut off that nagging inner voice that says there's something that you either should be doing or something that absolutely needs to get done and isn't? When you let go completely of the need to be productive in any way and you give yourselves this experience of relaxation, you are telling the universe that you desire more opportunities for these types of experiences.

And then there is the question of whether you would even accept an opportunity to slow down if it were granted to you by everyone around you. Would you accept the gift of doing nothing if it were offered to you? Or would you look for some way to prove your value and your worth, either to others or to yourself?

The simple act of closing your eyes, relaxing your body, and taking a few deep breaths will shift you on every level of your being. You will give yourself a mini-clearing every time you do it and you will find that your life becomes more meaningful, more satisfying, more manageable, and filled with opportunities to relax and enjoy it more.

We are Michael. We are infinite. We are Love."

SHIFTING IS EASY TO DO

∞

"Welcome. We are here to serve and assist you.

Blinking in and out of the physical reality is something that you do without realizing that you are doing it. You are not physical for exactly as long as you are physical. And this blinking gives you an opportunity to blink in to another reality. It is easier for you to shift to a parallel universe than you might think.

There is a practice of shifting realities that few have mastered, but those that have, understand the blinking in and out of the physical reality. They are simply keeping up with the speed of that blinking.

This is not something that you can do in order to escape a problem because as long as you are focused on a problem, you are incapable of keeping up with the very fast rate at which you are blinking in and out. This is something you can do when you are in a very high-vibrational state, when you are feeling light, carefree, and joyous.

Now, when you shift to another parallel universe, you will not necessarily know where you are going. But when you are in that state of being, you trust that where you are going is going to be of a similar vibration. And so you are not attached to shifting to a particular parallel universe.

And in that non-attachment, you make it possible. We are suggesting that you have fun with this, that you play around with it, and that you demonstrate to yourselves just how much fun you can have and just how easy it is to shift.

We are Michael. We are infinite. We are Love."

HONEST COMMUNICATION

∞

"Welcome. We are here to serve and assist you.

The way to an open and honest dialogue with another begins with the self. There is no honesty with another without first having that honesty within. The most truthful experience a person could ever have occurs when they are aware of how they feel.

Therefore, an honest conversation is a conversation about feelings. Who did what, what was said by whom, and even the intentions behind what was done and what was said pale in comparison to an open and honest conversation about feelings, emotions, frequency states.

Why is it so important for you to know how you feel, and why is it also important for you to communicate your feelings with another? The importance lies within the experience. Everything else on your world gives you the experience of the emotion, of the feeling, of the frequency. So none of it matters unless it evokes a response within you.

And when it does, that is worth noting, that is worth paying attention to, and that is worth talking about. You are Source Energy Beings having these experiences. This is fascinating stuff. This is significant.

These feelings are why you came. Everything else is there to get you to feel. Therefore, talking about the stuff, the words, the deeds, the situations, is like going to an art exhibit and only talking about the frames.

We are Michael. We are infinite. We are Love."

SYNERGY

∞

"Welcome. We are here to serve and assist you.

One in the presence of another can elicit more than an individual is capable of bringing forth by him- or herself. So coming together with another will always enable more of your essence to shine through. It is very much the synergy of your energy and the energy of one or more that creates higher and higher frequency states.

Now, we often tell you that you can go within and find everything that you could ever experience outside of yourselves. And so, we want you to know that we are not contradicting ourselves here. What we are talking about is still that energy flowing from within you. But we are also acknowledging that oftentimes it is another individual that stimulates that flow.

Also, we would like to point out that two individuals who are tapped in to their own flow of Source Energy is much more powerful than one person by him- or herself. And when you have two or more flowing the infinite abundance of Source Energy, the effect is more than just one plus one would indicate. The effect is exponential.

Therefore, we recommend coming together with others and shining your light while encouraging others to shine theirs. It can be a very selfish act to get together with another and to have that experience of the synergistic flow of your energy and the energy of the other.

Now, of course, the opposite also holds true. When you have more than one person blocking that energetic flow in the same room, the downward spiral is just as intense. So we suggest knowing when to walk away and knowing when the time is right for convening with others and having the blissful experience of allowing your highest frequency energy to flow while also bathing in the energetic flow of another.

We are Michael. We are infinite. We are Love."

YOUR METAMORPHOSIS

∞

"Welcome. We are here to serve and assist you.

Changing from within, this is all you ever do. It is what you experience your lives as. You cannot stop change from occurring, but you can resist it or allow it. You are on a never-ending journey of expansion and growth, and you cannot experience your growth and your expansion without also experiencing change.

Notice yourselves as you cling to what is familiar, not only about your surroundings and the people you associate with, but also in yourselves. You cannot be the same person from one moment to the next. It is simply not possible. So, as a new person, your only real concern must be, 'Who am I in this moment, and can I love and accept myself as I am?'

Who you were yesterday is irrelevant. Who you were ten years ago is but a distant memory. There is not one of you who benefits from clinging to any idea of who you have been prior to this moment. It not only does not serve you, it brings you less to be excited about.

You are changing more rapidly now than ever before, and the change that you experience is not as simple as a change in your address, your occupation, or your appearance. We are talking about a metamorphosis that will change everything, and we are asking you to trust that what you are changing into is more of what you have always known yourselves to be.

You cannot possibly get lost in this process. It is your destiny. And as you change, you bring new awareness to that which you have always been. With new awareness comes new perception. And with new perception comes a new reality. And with that new reality comes an even greater sense that you are complete and whole and becoming even more than you could have ever dreamed or imagined.

We are Michael. We are infinite. We are Love."

THE EXPANSION OF YOUR CONSCIOUSNESS

∞

"Welcome. We are here to serve and assist you.

There always is room for your consciousness to expand into something more. Your ability to experience more of reality depends upon your ability to allow that expansion to occur. And the way that you allow an expansion of consciousness to occur is by letting go.

By letting go of the need for anything in your current reality to be something other than what it is, you then lay down your resistance to it, which allows you to integrate it, to become it. And as you do, you get to move on to something else, some other aspect of your consciousness that is waiting for you to welcome it home.

Now, we understand why some of you are offering the resistance that you are. When you see something that you do not want, you then believe that you must resist it in order to resonate with what you do want and experience that instead. But you see, not resonating with and resisting are two very different things.

When you do not resonate with something, you do not have to worry about it becoming more of your experience. It cannot. And you can gravitate towards that which does resonate with you. Resistance on the part of any of you comes from the idea that something could impose its will upon you.

So recognizing your ability to create your reality, no matter what exists within it, will help you in softening your resistance to those things you do not resonate with. And then you will live in harmony and your expansion will be steady, easy, and filled with new experiences that you do desire to have.

We are Michael. We are infinite. We are Love."

A REASON TO EXIST

∞

"Welcome. We are here to serve and assist you.

From the beginning, there has always been a reason to exist for every single one of us. That reason has been expanded upon, but the reason itself has not changed. The reason for existence is to feel. Now, when we say 'feel,' we mean everything.

We are referring to your emotions, but we are also referring to frequencies, sensations, and the physical experience of feeling as well. To the extent that it is possible, we suggest that you dive deeply into every feeling, every sensation, and that you take a moment to check in more frequently.

Check in to see what frequency you are holding. The key in all of this is to feel without judgment, to feel without fear, fear that what you are feeling is inappropriate, wrong, or that it will get you some unwanted manifestation. Trust your feelings. Give in to your feelings. And most of all, feel your feel

See if you can do so without questioning where they originated from. See if you can have a pure experience of a feeling, as though you were an explorer, as though you were Source Energy getting to know itself in the most appropriate way possible.

And as you feel, become aware of every part of you and how every part of you is experiencing that feeling. We invite you to expand your consciousness beyond that of an ego while you experience a feeling so that you can know that no matter what the feeling is, there are many different ways to perceive it. And you, as the feeler of the feeling, are much more significant than it is.

We are Michael. We are infinite. We are Love."

THE SAME PEOPLE

∞

"Welcome. We are here to serve and assist you.

In the process of evolution, you often find yourselves meeting the same people over and over again, even if they are coming to you disguised in different bodies. You will continue to co-create with beings of the same frequency, who offer you the same challenges, until you come to a place where you can love and accept the being just as they are.

There is no escape in this universe. Now, that being said, you do get to decide when it is most appropriate for you to process what you need to process. And so, if you need to walk away from a person, then you are well within your rights to walk away, to regroup, and to face that particular challenging person in another form, at another time.

Some of your most productive time is spent by yourselves. And much of the time that you are by yourselves, you are processing what you need to from your interactions with other people, from your financial and health circumstances, and even from past life traumas. So if you find yourself spending the majority of your time by yourself, there is a very good chance that you are making the necessary adjustments in order to face your more challenging cohorts in the physical for another round.

You don't do it because of karma, and you don't do it because you have to in order to prove yourselves. You do it because you want to. You do it because you are unconditional love looking for ways to know yourselves completely and fully as that and only that.

We are Michael. We are infinite. We are Love."

YOU ARE ALWAYS MOVING FORWARD

∞

"Welcome. We are here to serve and assist you.

There is always motion forward, no matter how it may look. No matter what is occurring in your lives, you are moving forward in your evolution. This is excellent news for those of you who have been struggling in some area of your lives. You may wonder what you are doing wrong or how you are blocking yourself from getting to where you want to go.

But we are here to tell you that any stagnation that occurs in the physical is serving you spiritually. So instead of blaming yourselves for not moving forward, not getting closer to your desires, ask yourselves how it serves you to be right where you are with all of your apparent blockages.

Perhaps you need to surrender more to the apparent lack of progress in your lives. Perhaps you are giving yourself the opportunity to love yourself unconditionally. Perhaps you just want to have the experience of unconditional joy in your life.

Fulfilling whatever desire is out of reach for you would give you a reason to be excited and joyous and to love yourselves. But if you can do all of that without seeing any progress in the physical, then you will have demonstrated to yourself that you are more important than your desires. You and your happiness are significant, and they are significant enough to take priority over that which you desire.

We suggest that you slow down from time to time and look for something in your immediate experience to give thanks for, to explore, and to appreciate. And then congratulate yourself for having not only created it, but for also taking the time to enjoy it.

We are Michael. We are infinite. We are Love."

PROCESSING EMOTIONS

∞

"Welcome. We are here to serve and assist you.

Processing an emotion is not as cut and dried as you might think. It is not as though you get through the entire experience of that emotion in one sitting, and it is to your benefit that you don't take on the entirety of the experience all at once. So when you are processing an emotion, feeling it, breathing it, allowing it to be, you are in a sense training yourself.

And it serves you very well to not try to get past anything, or to do away with something once and for all. Instead, we invite you to experience every emotion as though it were the first time you were feeling it. It may seem like a familiar feeling, like something you have experienced many times before. But it will not be exactly the same, because you are never exactly the same.

So recognize your evolution, as the feeler of the emotion, as you allow that emotion to be processed through you. Give it your full and complete attention. See it always as coming to serve you and to deliver to you exactly what you need to know in the moment.

Once you have processed your emotions without fear or judgment, you are then able to sense the nuance within them. You are able then to experience them from a whole new perspective. You can begin to see them as your friends, your co-creators.

And when you do so, you will begin to syphon power from them, no matter what the emotion is. Whether it is positive or negative, it carries power within it, power that can be harnessed and utilized by you, the experiencer of the emotion.

We are Michael. We are infinite. We are Love."

COMPASSION & KINDNESS

∞

"Welcome. We are here to serve and assist you.

To address a situation with kindness and compassion means that you have already come to the resolution of whatever it is you are facing. You often focus on results, accomplishments, and getting the job done. But when you are faced with a challenging situation between yourself and another, or perhaps even just between yourself and you, as long as you are taking a compassionate and kind approach, you will have succeeded.

You don't create problems for yourselves so that you can have the mental experience of solving that problem or of reaching a resolution. You create those scenarios for yourselves to give yourselves an opportunity to respond with compassion and kindness. That is how you measure how far you have come. It is not by measuring the number of problems or difficult situations you have in your lives.

Make it your number one intention to deal with yourselves and others with kindness and compassion first. Do not be in such a hurry to find the solution or to come to the completion of the interaction. Instead, make room for more compassion, more kindness, and more love. If something remains unresolved, see it as a window of opportunity for you to show some more compassion, for you to offer some more kindness.

When you see everything in your lives as an opportunity to experience more of who you really are, then you welcome it all with open arms. You see the gift of it. And the more compassion you experience for others and yourselves in every situation, the more likely you then become to find yourselves living in a compassionate world, filled with kindness, filled with unconditional love, and with no need to eliminate problems.

We are Michael. We are infinite. We are Love."

THE EVOLUTION OF YOUR CONSCIOUSNESS

∞

"Welcome. We are here to serve and assist you.

Vibration is the natural state of being for all expressions of Source. You cannot stop vibrating, but it is possible to slow it down or to speed it up. Slowing it down gives you a denser experience of reality. Speeding it up gives you a lighter experience of reality.

You can see from that explanation that there is no right and no wrong. These are all choices that you make to give yourselves an experience of reality. This is why you will never experience judgment from Source. You will never experience judgment because the speed at which you choose to vibrate puts you in harmony with others who are vibrating at that speed. So you are all being given the opportunity to have an experience of that particular frequency of vibration.

And as you all decide that you want to raise your vibration, you get to have a different experience of reality, of yourselves, and of one another. Condemnation is of a lower vibration, and it will keep you stuck right where you are, having the same type of experience that you've been having.

And that is what makes acceptance, forgiveness, and letting go your ultimate pathways to a higher vibrational experience. And then you get to have a whole new reality with different versions of the same people that you once condemned. That is evolution.

That is the evolution of your consciousness, and that is inevitable. When you make this a conscious journey, however, you experience yourselves as creator beings. And that is truly the most satisfying experience of your evolution.

We are Michael. We are infinite. We are Love."

NON-LINEAR EVOLUTION

∞

"Welcome. We are here to serve and assist you.

Taking steps forward often requires you to experience what seem to be setbacks. That is just how it works in duality. When you have as much polarity as you do on your world, you will often give yourselves both the experience of a setback and the experience of moving forward. This is often confusing to you because you tend to believe that you are always and only moving in one direction or the other.

You tend to think that you can only be offering one vibration at a time, and therefore, can only experience one type of life circumstance at a time. What this experience does for you is that it gives you a taste of both ends of the spectrum, and this allows you to see more clearly the path ahead. You are also being given the opportunity to have a fuller experience of an idea or a concept. But it can be challenging for you to see the benefit in that. You tend to only see the benefit in moving forward, in moving closer to your goal, or your desire, or even the more evolved you.

When you are fifth-dimensional beings, you will understand more clearly how paths do not move in a linear way. You will understand more the ability for you to jump around and have no consistency whatsoever in what you experience. This can be very confusing to the mind and very scary to the emotional body. But look at it this way. If you wanted something to expand, wouldn't you want to push at the edges of it from every possible angle, not just one? You are expanding. You are becoming more. And the experience of moving forward and moving backwards and moving forward, gives you precisely what you need to expand and to burst free from the boxes you have created and labeled as 'good' and 'bad.' We invite you to discover who you are in the midst of these experiences, rather than simply measuring how close you are or how far you are away from those goals and desires that you want for yourselves.

We are Michael. We are infinite. We are Love."

BEING MORE SPIRITUAL

∞

"Welcome. We are here to serve and assist you.

Pretending that something does not bother you when it actually does is not an act of being more spiritual. You do not gain anything at all by trying to be who you are not. Who you are in any moment is precisely who you need to be in that moment. And if that means you are not okay with something that you believe you are supposed to be okay with, then you need to honor yourself in that moment.

You need to admit to yourself that you are feeling what you are feeling about it, even if it is not a very popular way to feel. There is a composite spiritual person that you all think about when you think of being more enlightened. This spiritual master is how you all aspire to be like.

And so at times you allow yourselves to be in denial, or you beat up on yourselves for not being there yet, for not living up to this ideal standard of the spiritual master, the enlightened one. But honoring yourself right where you are and giving yourself whatever it is you need is the most compassionate thing and the most loving thing that you could do. And being compassionate and loving with yourself is the spiritually evolved way to be.

So we recommend that you throw away your picture of that enlightened master and that you let go of any desire to be someone other than who you are. In so doing, you allow yourselves and others to live and let live in a beautiful place where each of you is perfect as you are. That type of harmony and peace can be achieved on Earth right here and right now. Not everyone must reach enlightenment before that happens.

We are Michael. We are infinite. We are Love."

WHAT IS SHIFTING

∞

"Welcome. We are here to serve and assist you.

All that you are is contained within the tiniest portion of you. There is no need for you to go anywhere or to become anything in order to access your Source and all of the energy and information that is contained within it.

We sometimes talk to you about your expansion and your growth, and we understand how that can give you the impression that you have you somewhere to go or that you are somehow less than your complete and whole self. What we really mean when we talk about expansion and becoming is your awareness of self.

Your awareness of who you are is what is shifting, and that is a very big deal. You are discovering that all of your limitations are nothing more than ideas that you have been exploring. These ideas were always part of the plan, and you have given them quite a bit of your attention over the many lifetimes that you have incarnated.

The ideas themselves are not bad. They are not to be demonized or squashed out with all of your mental gymnastics. They are simply to be seen as they are and for what they are. And you are taking your attention away from them because you are exploring new ideas and new ways of knowing yourselves.

This also holds true for the others on your planet and your planet itself. You have the opportunity to embrace something more, something different, and something new. And we are here to guide you in that direction. But you don't really need us or anyone else to remind you. All you need to do is to feel for it within you and to follow the light.

We are Michael. We are infinite. We are love."

TRANSCENDING POLARITY

∞

"Welcome. We area here to serve and assist you.

The encouragement that you seek from outside sources is no different than the criticism that you attempt to avoid. Whenever you are looking for someone or something outside of you to give you a sense of validation or worth, you are always going to get the opposite of that which you seek as well. You cannot receive just one side or one end of the spectrum. So know that if you go seeking one, you will find the other as well.

When you are addressing yourselves, you get to choose every time whether you give yourselves praise or whether you criticize. You choose from both ends of the polarity. They are both there. They are both allowed to exist as choice. But you get to choose which one.

Now, most of you are not doing this consciously. So you choose to give yourselves praise only when you feel you deserve it, and you choose to criticize yourselves when you feel you deserve that. But what if you made the choice to give that which you want to receive to yourselves no matter what? What if you allowed the choice for self-criticism to be there, and yet, you chose self-love, encouragement, and blessing yourselves?

There would be no need for any of you to justify that which you gave yourselves with some sort of accomplishment or desired result. You could give yourselves unconditional praise before doing something. And then perhaps you would no longer seek that praise, that love, and that encouragement from an outside source. This is how you free yourselves from duality, from polarity. This is how you live in the fifth dimension.

We are Michael. We are infinite. We are Love."

ABSOLUTION

∞

"Welcome. We are here to serve and assist you.

Absolution will not rid you of the emotion that you feel. Give up the need for anyone to give you their forgiveness. You can receive it and still feel the guilt, the shame, and the regret. So seek not absolution from anyone, including that which you see as God.

When you participate in an event and you perceive that your participation has resulted in others being harmed physically or emotionally, you have let yourself create an experience for the purpose of feeling what it would be like. The experience itself is not meant to define you. It is not meant to be replayed over and over in your mind. You do not need to undo anything that has been done.

But the emotions that you feel are significant. Sometimes feeling an emotion helps you recognize that you do not want to participate in that particular event ever again. And when you allow yourselves to feel the emotions, rather than seeking the forgiveness or to undo what has been done, you receive the full benefit from having participated in the event.

Moving forward, you will better decide which ways you desire to interact with your world and with others. Doing so from a place of guilt will only infuse all future actions with that guilt. So we encourage you to let go and to recognize that you do not need to attach yourself to anything that you have ever participated in.

We are Michael. We are infinite. We are Love."

YOUR PERSONAL UPGRADES & SHIFTS

∞

"Welcome. We are here to serve and assist you.

There is a large segment of the human population that is undergoing personal upgrades and shifts. You all get to decide exactly how and when you experience these upgrades and shifts. So even though you are going through an ascension process as a collective, you are not all in the same phase.

Some are holding space while others are having their transformations. Others are holding the lower frequencies that are necessary in a system of duality. That is very important for you to recognize when you see these beings who are acting out in a myriad of ways on your world. They are necessary, and they are doing their jobs.

You, on the other hand, are consciously doing your jobs by allowing yourselves to experience everything and by shifting your consciousness deliberately because you want to maintain a higher frequency. And, of course, you are also receiving assistance from the higher realms. We are aware of each and every one of you, and we are assisting whenever and wherever possible.

But you will experience your shift yourself. Therefore, none of us in the higher realms can tell you what to expect. We can't because we don't know. We don't know how you will respond to something. That is where you come in, and that is the fun part of the experience.

The most important thing you could do during this time is to choose to respond in a way that is a reflection of your highest and best intentions. And when you do, you will find the shift to be not only easy but also enjoyable.

We are Michael. We are infinite. We are Love."

COMMUNICATING WITH LOVED ONES

∞

"Welcome. We are here to serve and assist you.

By attending to your relationships, you are granting yourselves access to more of who you are. The more time you spend interacting with others, the easier it is for you to expand. And the more time you spend avoiding others, the smaller you get.

Your relationships are the perfect tools for giving you exactly what you need. But you do not always use them that way. You do not always see others as extensions of yourself, as pieces or aspects of your consciousness. And that is when the relationships become more challenging, less fun, less exciting, and less rewarding.

So we recommend tending to your relationships, and the best way to do that is through open and honest communication. You receive so much more when you interact with others, and you also give more of that which you are. And that is the ultimate experience of your relationship to any other. The more of yourself that you give, the less you need, the more content you feel, and the easier it then becomes to be by yourself.

Tending to your relationship with yourself gives you a deeper sense of who you really are. No one else can be a substitute or fill in the gap that sometimes exists when you do not tend to that relationship as well. And when you do, all other relationships become beautiful exchanges of loving energy.

We are Michael. We are infinite. We are Love."

RAISING YOUR VIBRATION

∞

"Welcome. We are here to serve and assist you

By listening to your own words, you can discover what vibration you are holding. Every action that you take is also a clue. Every emotion that you feel gives you an indication of your current vibration. And of course, the thoughts that you think resonate with your vibrational offering. The vibration that you offer is like the magic wand. When you wave the magic wand, everything in its path changes.

So how do you change your vibration? How do you wave the magic wand so that everything you experience becomes of that vibration? You can start by surrounding yourselves with that which is of a high vibration.

Putting yourselves in nature is the easiest way. Listening to music that resonates the vibration you want to hold is another very easy method. Wearing clothes that feel good on your body, spending time with your pets, taking a bubble bath – there are a myriad of ways that you can easily affect your vibration.

And once you find yourselves in a place where you feel that you have a firm grip on the magic wand, let yourselves feel the vibration that you want to offer. Let the vibration run up and down your chakras. Become the vibration that you want to see reflected back to you, that you want to feel in your emotions, that you want to speak, think, and act.

The easiest way for you to adjust your vibration is to pay attention to the vibration you're offering and to simply intend that you raise your frequency. It is that simple.

We are Michael. We are Infinite. We are Love."

RELATIONSHIPS AND YOU

∞

"Welcome. We are here to serve and assist you.

The dynamics of any relationship can shift at any time, creating a new type of relationship. This is true, regardless of the type of relationship you have with another. And it is also true of the relationship you have with yourself.

Everything is always shifting and changing in order to give you a new experience. So nothing, and no relationship, is ever meant to stay the same throughout all of eternity. We know that you like it when you see two people who get married stay together for decades of your time. That is very comforting to all of you because of the fear that can come up around being alone.

Your relationships are really about giving you what you need so that you can more closely examine your relationship to yourself. And since you are an ever-changing being, your relationship to yourself is in a constant state of flux.

It is ultimately up to you to decide how you want to relate to yourself, others, and your world. If you want stability in your relationships, then look within yourself for that stability. Give others the opportunity to grow and evolve and to change the dynamic of your relationship to them. That is truly how you live happily ever after.

We are Michael. We are infinite. We are Love."

UNCONDITIONAL LOVE

∞

"Welcome. We are here to serve and assist you.

Before you decide to incarnate into a physical human body, you explore many different options. And you choose the one that gives you the greatest opportunity for experiencing yourselves as unconditional love. That may mean that you incarnate into a very challenging situation, and it may also mean that you create challenging situations for yourselves as you move through the lifetime.

Without those challenges, you would not fully understand what it means to be unconditional love. So it is important for you to look around at your lives and to see where those opportunities are.

For many of you, the unconditional love that you seek to know yourselves as requires you to accept who you are and what you have done. All of you have created situations that would require you to forgive another person in order to then experience yourselves as unconditional love.

The greatest example that you have of unconditional love on your world is with your pets. They love you unconditionally. And so, you often decide to travel from lifetime to lifetime with a pet, or several pets, that will incarnate with you to remind you of the unconditional love that you are.

You also have planet Earth herself, although it is more challenging for you to see, and feel, and recognize that love, because it is so easy for you to take the Earth for granted and to not even acknowledge all of the gifts that she gives you every day. So before you set out to know yourselves as unconditional love, and to give unconditional love to yourselves and others, tune yourselves to the planet and the animals and learn from them what it is like to hold that frequency all the time.

We are Michael. We are infinite. We are Love."

RELAX

∞

"Welcome. We are here to serve and assist you.

Letting yourselves into a relaxed state, notice how easily your thoughts reflect that state of being. It will serve you very well to notice this and to notice the ease with which you can find a different state of being. Then, notice how quickly your thoughts adhere to the new state of being you have found.

Breathing will always assist you in finding the state of being that you prefer. Whenever you find yourselves seeking solace from thoughts that seem out of control, or from a state of being that hits you like a ton of bricks from out of nowhere, put your attention on your breath and reach for the frequency of relaxation.

When you calm yourselves down, your frequency rises up. And when you are relaxed, calm, cool, and collected, everything around you slows down to reflect that state of being.

You offer more of your thoughts, words, and actions from a place of feeling lack of control than many of you realize. When you demonstrate to yourselves how easy it is to relax and to calm your nerves, then suddenly the need to control dissipates and you find yourselves in the flow of your lives, seeking to love, serve, and appreciate without attachment to outcomes and without even needing to know what you will do in the next five minutes.

Make it your highest priority to be the calm in the midst of your life, which at times feels like a storm. And you will not only affect what it is that occurs in your life, but you will begin to notice the beauty in the chaos.

We are Michael. We are infinite. We are love."

ONE BIG SOUL FAMILY

∞

"Welcome. We are here to serve and assist you.

Belonging to a group gives you a feeling of connectedness, of inclusion, and of strength and power. Belonging is something that most of you are striving to do. There are groups of you gathering with similar intentions, beliefs, and vibrations, and you find yourselves feeling satisfied when you are amongst your groups.

We encourage you to look for your tribes, your soul families, and those whose frequencies resonate with your own. We also want you to belong to the greater community that is your planet and all of her inhabitants. You're all here at the same time because you are all a part of a group consciousness and your stories are linked together, no matter how different they may seem in this moment and no matter how far from your own beliefs and lifestyle someone else is finding themselves.

You are here removing barriers and lines of separation. You are establishing greater bonds with those on the other side of the planet and all places in between because of your internet, and your phones, and all of the ways that you have of experiencing each other. It is our suggestion to you that you get excited about this group of Earthlings that you are here with at this time, for you are truly all in this together. No soul will be left behind.

Whenever you gather in a group, and you recognize yourselves as working for the light, extend yourselves out to include those who are not working for the light, who are not aware of their Divinity, and who find your beliefs frightening. Reach out energetically because your hearts are all connected, your souls all belong together. And even if your minds disagree, your actions are quite different, and your vibrations are far from harmonious, you're all here in service to one another and to the greater goal of ascension.

We are Michael. We are infinite. We are Love."

ALL OF YOUR RELATIONSHIPS

∞

"Welcome. We are here to serve and assist you.

Linking yourself to another puts you in a co-creative dance together. The dance is what you would call your relationship. As you connect with another's energy, you are accessing different data within yourself then you have previously had access to.

Your work together as friends, family, or lovers will be to access what you need to access to give you the experiences that you need to have. It is always part of your evolution to be involved with another in any way. When you let yourselves be completely open and receptive to all that the relationship has to give you, you make progress along your path.

And sometimes the other person will come with you. And sometimes they will not. As much as you want to believe that you are responsible for each other, this is never actually the case. Having said that, please recognize that you are all here to exist as a collective and to honor each other. That is quite different from being responsible for another's journey, happiness, or wellbeing.

As you continue along your path with the others that are joining you, give yourself exactly what you need and let the others do the same for themselves. Participate in the dance, but do not mistake the dance for what you are doing here. You always have the opportunity to extract what you need while giving more of who you are.

And that is quite different from giving all of your time, energy, and money. That is truly what you offer each other whenever you are in a type of partnership. You offer more of who you are, and you invite the other to do the same.

We are Michael. We are infinite. We are love."

MASTERY

∞

"Mastery does not come through repetitive action. That is a skill, not mastery. Mastery comes in the moment that you let all that you are participate in what you are doing. That can be done in an instant. That does not require you to do, or to repeat, until you get it just right.

So mastery happens in an instant, and you recognize mastery when you feel the vibration that has been infused into something. Elevating your skill level is a process that can be never-ending. You can get better, and better, and better at doing something, but there will always be more that you can do. There will always be more to that journey.

Achieving mastery in an instant, in a moment, needs no encore performance. You give yourselves opportunities for mastery all day, every day. Any time you are speaking, any time you are doing even the most mundane task, you have the opportunity to call forth more of yourself and to infuse more of yourself into what you are doing or saying.

And then you just let it be whatever it is. Whatever you say, you say. Whatever you do, you do completely. And you are the master who knows himself or herself as that moment, as that experience. You surrender to whatever comes through you, to whatever comes out of you, because you know that the true master never judges.

The true master never compares. The true master simply is fully and completely participating with no expectation, with no attachment to outcome, and with the knowing that everything that you are can be expressed in a single moment.

We are Michael. We are infinite. We are Love."

BUILD YOURSELVES UP

∞

"Welcome. We are here to serve and assist you.

By appreciating the value that you give to your world, to your species, and to all that exist, you find value in what others are offering as well. You exemplify that which others can aspire to feeling for themselves. Therefore, we see no harm whatsoever in building yourselves up, bragging even.

We want you all to know your value, and we want you all to experience it firsthand. We encourage you to express it without fear of being called selfish, arrogant, or narcissistic. By tooting your own horn, so to speak, you are delivering high frequencies to all who exist. You are setting the example to others of how to love oneself, how to see oneself as beautiful, as valuable, and as providing service.

You all want to feel valuable, and yet, you often deflect the compliments and the praise that you receive from others. And you wouldn't dare speak your own accolades publicly. And so we are suggesting that you start small. Simply acknowledge yourselves to yourselves. No one else has to be in earshot. Walk with your heads held high and believe in your value.

And as you do, you will see the value that others provide and it will be easier for you to praise them. There is an evolution that is well under way that includes every single one of you, no matter where you are today. And one of the paths to experiencing that evolution is acknowledging all the areas in yourself that are praiseworthy.

All we are asking is that for a few moments you focus on yourselves through the eyes of Source.

We are Michael. We are infinite. We are Love."

THE PROCESS OF PROCESSING
∞

"Welcome. We are here to serve and assist you.

Processing occurs on many different levels of your being-ness. Most of you start out by processing something mentally. You want things to make sense. You want to understand. Next, you have an emotional processing of an event, or of certain information.

The emotional processing is usually where you get stuck, and sometimes you go back and forth between the mental and the emotional processing. And this is how certain circumstances become patterns for you. It is so that you can move past the mental and the emotional processing.

If you move past emotional processing, you often move through a physical release. This you sometimes experience as tears or laughter, even a smile. Finally, you have an energetic processing. This is where integration occurs. This is where the work that you have done pays off.

It is like getting a part of yourself back as your energy field becomes clearer, less dense, and more open. When you are open energetically, you are far more receptive and far more creative. You step into your creative being-ness.

So what we are suggesting here is that you take note of where you are in the processing process. Notice when you are stuck and make it your intention to allow the process to go smoothly and without your interference. Being willing to process means being willing to let go of control. Instead, you want to become the experiencer of the process, the experiencer of your evolution, and of your ultimate ascension.

We are Michael. We are infinite. We are Love."

RECOGNIZING YOUR VALUE

∞

"Welcome. We are here to serve and assist you.

Recognizing your value involves less effort than you might think. Recognizing your worth is as simple as letting yourself off the hook. As soon as you decide that you need to measure up in some way, or to be better in some way than another, you are putting yourself in a position to not feel that value and that self-worth.

So we suggest that you give yourself credit for merely existing and that you see yourself as bringing something that only you can to this universe. You have your unique perspective and that is something worth acknowledging. No one else gets to be you. And therefore, your value comes inherent in your existence.

What you are here to do is to not prove your value. What you are here to do is to experience your value, and only you can do it. It is nice to receive compliments from others. It is nice to win awards, receive accolades, and so on. But none of that will ever replace what you can give to yourself.

You always have the opportunity to step into your uniqueness, to celebrate who you are, and to be the perfect you that you always are. Nothing can make you worthy or valuable, nothing you do, nothing that anyone can give you. Because if that were true, then they could also take it away, or you could somehow fail, and that simply is not possible because you already exist.

We are Michael. We are infinite. We are Love."

REMOVING LIMITATIONS

∞

"Welcome. We are here to serve and assist you.

When there are no limitations placed upon you, you experience yourself in the flow. You experience your life as a beautiful unfolding of events. Now, the limitations that we are speaking of are not the agreements that you have made for this physical realm. We are talking about limitations that you place upon yourselves in order to make sense of your lives.

The limitations of needing things to be a certain way and only accepting one form of a desire are two of the primary ways in which you distance yourselves from being in the flow. These are also limitations that are easily released. But the first step is in noticing when you are placing these limitations on yourselves.

So let us say that you want to go on a trip to an exotic location, and you tell yourself that you must first gather three thousand dollars in order to afford the airfare and accommodations. That is a limitation that you are placing on all the different probable realities that exist, that could lead you to being in that location, having the experiences you want to have.

So become aware of these types of limitations so that you can let go and let in the experience that you really want to have. Once you find yourself in a state of desire, the only thing left to do is to let go and to appreciate the journey.

All you need to do is stop struggling in order to make it happen in the precise way that you have determined it must. When you take these simple steps, you remove limitations, and you live life in the flow.

We are Michael. We are infinite. We are Love."

CLEARING COLLECTIVE KARMA

∞

"Welcome. We are here to serve and assist you.

We are very pleased to announce to all of you that there has been a shift in your collective consciousness that has taken place over the past several days. You are releasing yourselves from collective karma on your world. And this is very exciting for us to report.

You may wish to look around inside yourselves and feel for some of your old guilty emotions. We think you will find that they are no longer there. How could you do this as a collective? We know that all of you have an awareness of events that occur outside of your communities. You cannot help but overhear someone talking about wars and other conflicts around your globe.

Even if you attempt to cover your ears and avert your eyes, you are aware of conflict, and war, and violence. You do not need to participate, physically, in these conflicts in order for their effects to ripple through you. Those effects are the mechanisms by which you are clearing collective karma, for you have all been engaged in wars and struggles on massive scales. And you all feel pain at times, not only because of what is going on out there, but because of what those events trigger in all of you. You may not even realize it is happening, but that guilt and that judgment rises to the surface. Your minds give you stories about what these feelings are about.

And, of course, you are not going to recall every single lifetime and everything that has transpired. That would be too big of a distraction and would actually take you away from feeling the feelings. So give yourselves some credit here for having done this work, for having let go.

Breathe a collective sigh of relief and let your brothers and sisters know, vibrationally, around the world that their work is now done. You can begin to notice now the peace within you. And as you do, you will see changes in what is occurring all around your globe.

We are Michael. We are infinite. We are Love."

GOING BIG

∞

"Welcome. We are here to serve and assist you.

Before you take a step forward in your life, you often think about where you might go, where that step might ultimately lead you. There comes a moment where you must decide, one way or the other, one direction or the other. And that decision point becomes more important and more significant with every choice that you make.

You are at the high stakes tables now. There is no more playing small for any of you, because your life simply will not allow it. Now we give you this information not so that you will put more pressure on yourselves when making decisions about your lives. We tell you this because we want to encourage you to reorganize your priorities if you have not done so already.

So here's what looking small would be in this current day and age. You would give in to mediocrity. You would settle. You would play it safe in every aspect of your life. Going big, by comparison, means that you are following your feelings. You are never weighing pros and cons, and you are always looking at the biggest possible picture.

The biggest possible picture is always your evolution, because you are here to become more of who you are. And any decision you make that supports the becoming of more of who you are will lead you in a direction that is far more satisfying. Your lives are getting bigger all the time. You are expanding your awareness of who and what you are. You are making connections with other beings, physical and non-physical, from other dimensions.

You cannot fit into the box that society has laid out for you anymore. We sense that more and more of you are breaking free from those boxes, and we want you to know that you have our support any time you make a decision that will result in the becoming of more of who you are.

We are Michael. We are infinite. We are Love."

ENLIGHTENMENT

∞

"Welcome. We are here to serve and assist you.

The way to enlighten yourself is to allow more of that which you are to rise to the surface. You will become conscious of all that you are, and you are doing so bit by bit and piece by piece. Your attempts to keep parts of yourselves hidden are failing.

The clearest path to enlightenment is recognizing that parts of yourself that are emerging are not always doing so from within. You will serve yourselves by acknowledging that the others in your world are also those bits and pieces, and they will continue to make themselves known to your conscious awareness until you love and accept them just as they are.

Your deliberate attempts at welcoming these aspects of yourselves into the fold of who you are will save you the necessity of doing so from an unconscious state. You value your individuality and you value the choices that you make -- choices that you believe define who you are. And that is why accepting others as parts of you is one of the more challenging obstacles that you have placed before you.

But you know that you can do it, and you know that it is the only game in town. And so, you are going to integrate all of the bits and pieces, and you are going to acknowledge that whatever you see is in some way a reflection of your whole self. The only question is: when and how. And that is up to you.

Our recommendation is to seek compassion for yourselves, no matter what you have done or not done and to offer others the same. Enlightenment can be a bit messy, but you are the ones that you sent to clean up the mess.

We are Michael. We are infinite. We are Love."

YOUR PERFECT JOURNEY

∞

"Welcome. We are here to serve and assist you.

In your journey of evolution, there is not one turning point that makes all the difference. You do not need to worry about making a wrong turn or a wrong decision that would somehow thwart your progress. The journey that you are on is not about finding the right way, or the right thing to do, not at any moment, and not as a long and drawn out path.

All that really matters is that you show up. When you show up for your life, you give yourselves the opportunity for experience. And experience is what the Oversoul craves. So from the Oversoul's perspective, there's nothing you could ever do to screw up on your journey. There is no point of no return, and there is no such thing as a mistake.

When you recognize that at the heart of your journey is you as the experiencer, then you are less likely to measure yourselves or to count your worthiness by how many good deeds you did, how much you avoided temptation, or how often you meditated. You get to be the one at the heart and soul of your journey.

And as you are that being, the one having the experiences, you get to decide in every moment which version of yourself you want to be. And that is not dependent upon anything that you have or have not done, said, or experienced up until the point of decision. You get to decide, not your past, not your past lives, not even your Oversoul. And every decision that you make is perfect, just like you.

We are Michael. We are infinite. We are Love."

The Third Sign

∞

You Are Receiving More Than You Ever Have Before

LISTEN TO YOUR LIFE
∞

"Welcome. We are here to serve and assist you.

Living this moment is all you need to focus on. Being aware in the moment will give you everything that you need to know. Giving your complete self to a moment is all that will ever be asked of you within it. Set your sights on what is in front of you and give it your complete attention, your complete awareness, and your complete self.

Listen to your life. Have you noticed that your life is speaking to you? There are times when you will find that it is easier to unravel and decode the messages of your life. And there will be times when what your life is telling you is so obvious that you would literally have to close your eyes and cover your ears to ignore it.

Let your life tell you what the moment is all about for you. If you are willing and able to stay within the moment to listen to what you are getting and to relax, you will have no more problems, issues, or life catastrophes. You will be able to unlock all the mysteries, all that has been eluding you. And all the excuses that you have been using to not live the life you want to live will wither away and turn to dust.

'Is it really that simple?' you might wonder. Well, everything is simple and easy if you allow it to be and if you allow it to be whatever it is without resistance.

We are Michael. We are infinite. We are Love."

UNLOCKING YOUR ABILITIES

∞

"Welcome. We are here to serve and assist you.

The inner workings of the human being are quite complex. You are intricate beings. So much so that your scientists have only begun to understand how it is that you truly interact with your world. Your brains are mostly a mystery. What makes you all tick and what makes your hearts beat has less to do with physiology and more to do with spirit, and with will, with consciousness, and with intention.

So given your complex and intricate nature, you must be capable of much more than you have ever imagined. Everything that you need is already inside of you. That is why it is very puzzling to those of us who watch over you when we see you place so much emphasis on technology getting you to where you want to go.

By unlocking the abilities within you, you are able to access vast amounts of power and creativity. All that you are and all that you seek pales in comparison to the ability that you have to love. Love is not complicated, intricate, or complex. And it just so happens to be the fuel for all of these abilities you are unlocking and uncovering.

What is it that allows the 98-pound woman to lift the car when her son or daughter is trapped underneath? What is it that gives you the energy to continue on with what you are passionate for when you haven't slept or eaten in 18 hours? What is it that gives you the ability to heal? It is always love. Love is the fuel and love is what propels you into higher frequencies.

Love is what unlocks your abilities, giving you more of who you really are and allowing you to play on a much bigger scale. And when you decide that Love is what you are all about, you step into a potential that will take you into the fifth dimension.

We are Michael. We are infinite. We are Love."

BE RECEIVERS

∞

"Welcome. We are here to serve and assist you.

Someone has let you off the hook in your life, and you have put yourself back on it. This happens whenever you decide that you do not deserve something. And when you feel that you do not deserve something, then even when it is being given to you, you deny it.

You want to live in harmony with this universe, and there is no struggle or earning when there is harmony. We suggest letting yourselves off the hook more often, if for no other reason than to practice accepting a gift, a break, an opportunity that comes to you from out of the blue. Letting go of the need to justify what comes to you will set you free.

Even those of you who have let go of the notion that you must work hard to receive compensation have adopted a new way of limiting how much you are willing to receive. You have been told about the law of attraction, vibration, and frequency, and now you are using that as a way of measuring how good you are at manifesting and creating the reality that you prefer.

We suggest that you let go of needing to justify through your vibration, your thoughts, and your emotions. Let yourselves be receivers of all that comes to you. Be thankful, and let that be the vibration that brought it to you in the first place.

We are Michael. We are infinite. We are love."

RESOURCES

∞

"Welcome. We are here to serve and assist you.

You give yourselves what you need. You have much more than you realize. If you are experiencing shortage of any kind it is only because you have not allowed yourself to see everything that is available to you and to see it in its fullest form and greatest value. You are one of those resources.

You have much more potential than you allow yourselves to realize. You have opportunities that are given to you to demonstrate how many resources you actually have. Seizing the opportunity is as simple as widening the scope of your perspective.

When you are struggling, and clenching your fists, and gritting your teeth, you are narrowing your perspective, and you are unable to see all of the resources that are available to you. When you relax, let go, and open yourselves to possibilities that may not fit in your idea of perfection, you are then able to not only see the resources that are all around you, but you are able to utilize them with ease and grace and joy.

Instead of asking for something that you feel you are lacking, ask to be shown more of the gifts that are all around you, waiting to be discovered by you. And recognize yourselves as the biggest resources, the greatest gifts, and the most honored and revered beings. And you shall receive all that you need.

We are Michael. We are infinite. We are love."

YOUR CREATIVE PROCESS

∞

"As you create, you extract data – data that will be used in your creation. You are keepers of records. You are like giant hard drives, and you access the data that you need when it is appropriate. You do not open your computer and have every single file on the screen in front of you. You access the ones that you need.

You do the same when it comes to your process of creation. You do not have a set of rules that you follow or steps that you take. The process is automatic. When you speak, you form words into sentences without thinking about the precise order of those words, and you do not carefully select every word in most conversations. You open your mouth and you let it flow, and the data that is necessary simply comes to you.

The same is true in your creative process, but you do not always allow the process. The more you struggle, the more you try to figure out, the less data you access. The more in the flow you are with your life, the more the data flows. And suddenly you know things that seem to come from out of the blue. You have insights, ideas, and new discoveries that come to you.

But where do they come from? Where was that information yesterday? It comes when it is relevant and when it is needed. Not a moment before and not a moment after. First, believe that what we are saying is true. And then live your life with that knowing, that everything is coming to you at the perfect time, when you will be able to utilize it for your highest good. And give your minds a rest so that the data can come from the broader you.

We are Michael. We are infinite. We are Love."

OPEN YOURSELVES TO MORE

∞

"Welcome. We are here to serve and assist you.

Starting with the premise that you are all Source Energy, open yourselves to more. Open yourselves to more of that which you are. You are capable of being so much more and of handling and distributing so much energy. And when you release any need to control the pathways through which energy will flow to you, you will notice a very steady increase.

When you give yourselves permission to receive and you are not fixated on one particular avenue from which the energy must flow, you light up new circuitry within your field. New receptors are born. You are able then to download frequencies that will be the catalyst for you to integrate more of that which you call Source into your bodies, into your fields, into your activities, and into your thoughts.

As you all ascend into the higher realms, you set yourselves on a course that contains more of that which you call love, light and all that you imagine is good. Get comfortable with the higher frequencies. Get aligned with them. Do not retract in the same way that do from lower frequencies and from pain. Open yourselves bravely and courageously to receive more of that which you are.

And let it be integrated, just as you are integrating the lower frequencies that have been the cause for much pain, suffering, and shame in your lives. We encourage you to open the floodgates and to do so consciously, willingly, and knowingly, accepting all that you are and knowing that you will know exactly what to do, and exactly what to say, and exactly how to utilize this energy.

We are Michael. We are infinite. We are Love."

THE HAVES AND THE HAVE-NOTS

∞

"Welcome. We are here to serve and assist you.

Monetarily speaking, there is more now than ever. There is no shortage on your world. There is only the perception of shortage. This perception of shortage is responsible for the increasing gap between 'haves' and 'have-nots.'

Perceiving a shortage does not necessarily create shortage in one's experience. That is how the 'haves' manage to accumulate so much. So it is not only a belief in shortage that creates a shortage in one's experience. So what is the reason then why the same belief can create abundance in the experience of some and lack in the experience of so many others?

It is always about the feeling that ensues as a result of the belief that is held. Most respond to that particular belief with struggle and despair. And a few, relatively speaking, respond with determination and desire. Desire that springs from a knowing within will always be met with an alignment of what is desired and the person offering the knowing.

Desire that is combined with a feeling of helplessness will fan the flames of the desire but will not result in an alignment with what is desired. So when you are considering your financial situation, be willing to examine everything that comes up within you and know that there is not a right way or a wrong way to feel in regards to your finances.

Let yourselves off the hook. Be willing to be where you are. And know that fortunes change as easily as you allow them to.

We are Michael. We are infinite. We are Love."

GIVING AND RECEIVING

∞

"Welcome. We are here to serve and assist you.

To give and release all expectation for gratitude or reciprocation is one of the many ways you have of knowing yourselves as Source Energy. Giving places value upon not only that which is given, but also upon the person who receives. When you give the gift, you give another a sense that they are worthy, that they matter, and that they are loved.

Truly, there is no greater way of knowing yourselves as abundant than to give something that you have that feels valuable to you. Make no mistake about it – the real gift that you have to give is that of your true essence. But sometimes you have the opportunity to give something physical, something that another could use. And that is wonderful as well.

By letting another give to you, you also give a gift. You give the gift of receiving and allowing the other to feel their benevolence and abundance. You often come to a place in your lives where you have more than enough, and you are presented with the opportunity to either cling to what you have or to give some of it away. We are not telling you that you must give. Because if you are not feeling abundant, then giving what you have only amplifies that feeling.

So many of you are witnessing a shift in the way that you exchange energy on your world. You want to be a part of that shift. And one of the easiest ways to do that is to give without expectation of receiving anything in return. That is much more effective than any demonstration you could partake in that is designed to point out the corruption or greed that is prevalent on your world. Be the change. Show others that there is another way.

We are Michael. We are infinite. We are Love."

PRAYER

∞

"Welcome. We are here to serve and assist you.

We always appreciate your prayers. Your prayers are coming from your most heartfelt desires, and we appreciate that you take your time to reach out. We understand that all of you are looking for help and are looking for answers.

We are anticipating that which you are asking for, before you even decide to relay the prayer. We are giving you an opportunity to hear yourselves as you say your prayers and as you make your requests. We are already giving you the answers to your prayers in the moment that your desire is created.

However, you may still want to ask. You may still want to give voice to your desires, for they are a part of you. They are coming from a deep place within you. Your feeling is what is transmitted in the prayer. The words are not part of our expression. We are not verbal and we do not have language.

But we feel you, and we know the essence of what you are asking for, and that is always what you are being given. You are the answerers of your own prayers. You are giving yourselves an opportunity to experience what it is like to move from having a desire to having the desire fulfilled. That is one of the reasons why you exist where you do and how you do.

We are holding your frequency here in the angelic, and we are watching like proud parents as you catch up, as you make your journeys, and as you know yourselves as the answerers of your own prayers.

We are the Archangel Michael. We are infinite. We are love."

DESIRE
∞

"Welcome. We are here to serve and assist you.

The story that you are telling begins with your desire. You have many desires, and no story even gets off the ground without some desire spurring it on. Having your desire fulfilled does not bring your story to an end, but it may be the end of a particular chapter.

Any desire worth its weight will spur on several more, and those desires may be put on the back burner while you continue to explore the desire that has most of your intention. You will discover that there is no end to the number of desires that you can have. Placing limitations or judgments upon your desires will not remove them from your being-ness.

You will not be able to trample your desire away with thoughts about how inappropriate it may be. You will discover more about yourself because of each unique desire. Truly, that is their purpose to you. You are not here simply to set goals and achieve those goals with your hard work and your determination.

You are here to explore who and what you are, and everything that you encounter is an avenue into more of yourself. Be willing to let your desires run free, but know what they really are about so that you do not mistake the desire for its ultimate purpose -- becoming more of who you are and becoming aware that what you are is Divine and is Love in action.

We are Michael. We are infinite. We are Love."

LISTEN AND RECEIVE

∞

"Welcome. We are here to serve and assist you.

Always listen because what is coming to you energetically can always be translated in some way, shape, or form. Give yourselves the opportunity to hear, to interpret, to know, and you will find that the more you listen, the more you are sent.

When you decide that you already have everything that you need and that there is nothing more for you to receive, you not only close off yourselves energetically, but you stop asking. We enjoy very much when one of you paints yourself into a corner, and you find that the only way out is to ask. You will always draw forth more when you allow yourselves to ask, and you will only hear when you listen. You will only receive when you open yourselves up.

As you encounter information be willing to give it a once over, no matter who the information seems to be coming from. If you will not listen because you assume that the person giving you the information is just a person or has a poor track record, then you will close off that avenue. You will make it that much more challenging for you to receive.

But if you understand that the entire Universe, and everyone and everything in it is just you interacting with you, then you will allow for multiple channels to give you exactly what you are asking for. We recommend that you set aside some time in your day to open yourselves up, and to listen, and to allow whatever is coming to come in whatever form it may.

We are Michael. We are infinite. We are Love."

YOU AND YOUR HELPERS

∞

"Welcome. We are here to serve and assist you.

The beings that wish you the greatest joy, love, and freedom are in many ways your ancestors and in many ways they are future versions of that which you are. You come from and to this plane of reality with a beautiful entourage of beings. You call them your guides and your angels, but they are so much more than that.

These are not just beings that care about and love you. These are pieces of your very consciousness that are looking in on that which they are, that which they were, and that which they will be. It is quite a process, this evolution of yours. It is not so cut and dried. There are many paths, many avenues, but one result.

And you are deciding which path, and they are watching you make those decisions and lending a hand when they can. They are not above you. They are not better than you. They have just as much to learn from you as you do from them. You are much more of a team than you realize.

You give them thanks and you seek their counsel. But we suggest that you see them more as a team – a team where you have your role as well, where you play your part. We suggest that you begin to see them as equals, that you look at your life as a project and you see them as contributing to the project. But you have as many answers as they do.

They will come to you for advice, for suggestions, and you will be of value and of service to them, for nothing in this universe is a one-way street. So before you ask for their help, their guidance, their answers, be willing to share something with them about your experience. Begin a dialogue. Give as much of yourselves to them as they have been and will continue to give to you.

We are Michael. We are infinite. We are Love."

SURRENDERING TO THE LIGHT

∞

"Welcome. We are here to serve and assist you.

Take yourselves beyond where you have been willing to dream or imagine that you could possibly go, and witness yourselves doing this from a place of knowing that it is your destiny. It is not a question of whether you will evolve and become more of who you are. The only question is, how far are you willing to go? How much love and how much light are you willing to hold within you?

That is truly the only limitation that is still on the table. You will exceed your wildest expectations for yourselves when you let go of any need to be in control of this process. When you surrender to it, when you give in to the light and the love that is pouring into you, you will go beyond what your minds can currently comprehend.

When we say 'surrender,' we are talking about surrendering control. We are talking about surrendering limitation. We are talking about no longer playing it small when it comes to your concept of who and what you are, what you are capable of, and how much light and love you can integrate into your being-ness.

Imagine yourselves enveloped in light, overcome and overpowered by Love, and see what kind of life you can live when you do. Give yourselves full access to all of the energy that is coming your way by simply surrendering to it, and let go of the need to know where it will take you. And when you do, you will discover new horizons, and you will live heaven on Earth.

We are Michael. We are infinite. We are Love."

YOU AND YOUR DESIRES

∞

"Welcome. We are here to serve and assist you.

Anyone would rather be sacrificed for what they desire than be forced to live in a way that is not in alignment with their desires. And you confirm this day after day by sacrificing yourselves for your desires in the hopes that those desires will fulfill you, bring you peace, and give you the life you've always dreamt of. As we witness you putting yourselves beneath your desires, we notice that not one of you takes a moment to question whether that desire is actually worth all of the hard work and all of the sacrifice.

We are not here to tell you that desires are bad or that they are beneath you. We are just sharing our observations about how you hold yourselves prisoner to those desires that always seem just out of reach. We would love to free you from that bondage, but we cannot do it by simply granting you all that you seek and strive for. But we would if we could.

We would rather direct you back to yourselves, and we would like to remind you that you desired nothing more for this incarnation than to be you, precisely and exactly as you are. We want to reawaken within you that primal desire to incarnate in your body for the sole purpose of being the unique expression that you are. We would love nothing more than for all of you to awaken to the realization that you are still the top priority for this incarnation.

And we want you to enjoy your desires, not for what they are, but for what they give you. They give you a reason to be here, expressing yourselves. And as you recognize that nothing short of the full expression of who you are will do, then your desires will be like the prizes that you get, rather than your reason for living.

We are Michael. We are infinite. We are Love."

WHAT DESIRES DO FOR YOU

∞

"Welcome. We are here to serve and assist you.

By giving yourselves that which you desire, you are setting yourselves free. As long as you are giving your power away to that which exists outside of you, you are in bondage. Now, we love that you have desires, and we encourage you to continue seeking out those pieces of your life that you want to see and feel and touch. But when your desires consume you, that is when they do not serve you.

When it becomes more important to you to obtain that which you desire than it does for you to feel free, happy, and peaceful, that is when you know that you have an unhealthy and unproductive relationship with that which you desire. Ask yourselves what you would be willing to do to have that which you desire. Your answer will tell you what your relationship to that desire really is.

Now when it comes to being and embodying that which you desire, that is something that requires you to do absolutely nothing. You already be, so there is nothing to do in order to become that which you already are. Becoming tuned to that which you desire is not about attracting it to you or manifesting it. It is about showing yourselves that you already are it and that in the knowing of yourselves as that which you desire, you are free.

You will only find enslavement where you give your power away. Reclaim your power by simply tuning in to the frequency of all that you desire and lighting up your world and everything in it with the intensity of your energy. That is how you benefit from having a desire in the first place.

We are Michael. We are infinite. We are Love."

MONEY

∞

"Welcome. We are here to serve and assist you.

Buying your life with currency is like taking a picture of something and then asking the picture to be the thing that it was only meant to represent. You have an expression that you cannot buy happiness. But still many of you seek to have more, assuming that the more will give you that which you have always sought.

Measuring the quality of life, or the standard of living, by keeping track of how much money is flowing is giving you a very biased perspective on what 'quality of life' actually means. Money is a form of exchange, and yet, it represents so much more to all of you. It represents freedom and security and power and status, and that is what you all have decided that money should represent.

But the poor man knows freedom in a way that the wealthy man does not. Children have very little money to spend, and yet, they are the happiest, most creative beings you'll ever come across. We are not attempting to discourage you from having money, but we want you to recognize that the money itself is not really what you seek.

And as you make your lives easier by reminding yourselves that the money itself is not what you are after, you'll notice how much power there is in not needing something. Exercise your sense of freedom by exploring all the things in your life that do not cost a dime. Make those things that which give you power, status, and stability, and notice how then money simply becomes something you play with for fun.

We are Michael. We are infinite. We are Love."

YOUR FUTURE

∞

"Welcome. We are here to serve and assist you.

In case you were wondering, there is nothing for you to worry about. In case you were having some doubts about the future, your future, and the future of the world, you can set your mind at ease. You can rest assured that everything is being taken care of. You can let go of any need to control or know about your future. We invite you to see that which lies ahead of you as you do Christmas morning. When you wake up on Christmas morning, you understand that there are gifts that you will enjoy, but you do not know what those gifts are. Everything that you desire, and everything that ultimately serves your greatest and highest good, is being wrapped up in a pretty package with a bow.

Now you may have to wait till Christmas morning, but you can rest assured that the gifts are there, your requests have been received, and all is going according to plan. Have you ever noticed that the best things in life come when you don't expect them, when you haven't lifted a finger, or tried to make any of it happen? And if you haven't noticed, then we suggest that you take an inventory and demonstrate to yourselves that what we are saying is true.

The more you recognize how wonderfully and easily everything is unfolding for you, the less worry and doubt you carry and the more you enjoy the gifts. But if you worry about whether or not the gifts are coming, all you do is trade your eager anticipation for fear.

We are not giving you this message because there is something wrong with worry and doubt. They are completely valid experiences for all of you. We are giving you this message so that you know you have a choice. The doubt, the worry and the fear will always be there too. But from this point forward we offer you the option of knowing, and we suggest you give it a try.

We are Michael. We are infinite. We are Love."

PLEASURE

∞

"Welcome. We are here to serve and assist you.

Pleasure comes in many forms. You have many ways of experiencing pleasure. You could say that it is a driving force for most of humanity. It is built in to your DNA to seek out pleasure and to avoid pain. The physical sensation of pleasure is often accompanied by the emotional state as well. You could call it joy, bliss, ecstasy, or something else.

Even though the physical sensation of pleasure has come first most of the time, we want to offer you another approach. In this approach that we are suggesting you seek out the emotional, the vibrational, the energetic experience of pleasure and you allow it then to be experienced as a physical sensation.

This is the inherent difference between going within and seeking that which is seemingly outside of yourselves. This pursuit of pleasure, however, does not require a lot of money, another person, food, or any of the other ways in which you seek out that experience of pleasure, and our suggestion gets you tapped in to the infinite source.

And when you are tapped in to the infinite source, suddenly you find yourselves not needing much of anything. And as your lives become simpler and easier, you find yourself in more of a state of bliss, or ecstasy, as a natural consequence of your existence, rather than because you found, or got your hands on, something outside of you that can only give you that temporary experience.

So we suggest giving yourselves the experience of pleasure without doing anything or seeking anything. And when you do, you will know yourselves as supremely powerful beings.

We are Michael. We are infinite. We are Love."

RECEIVING FROM ALL ANGLES

∞

"Welcome. We are here to serve and assist you.

The avenue through which you expect something to come to you is often not the path. And as long as you are pinning all of your hopes on it coming to you through that particular avenue, you are closing your eyes to the myriad of ways in which that same thing could find its way to you.

Oftentimes you not only expect that something will arrive through the route that you have selected for it, but you also have an attachment to it coming in that particular way. Let us use money as an example. Let us say that you want to get paid for doing something that you enjoy doing. And so the money serves multiple purposes for you, because if it comes to you in direct exchange for having done what you love to do, then you feel validated. You often need validation to come in order to keep you doing what you love to do.

So, what if instead you did what you love to do and you allowed money and other ways of supporting you to come from wherever the path was easiest for it to come? Could you then see the link between you doing what you love to do and you being supported? Could you see the link between the energy that you put out while you do what you love to do and the energy that comes back to you in the form of financial support?

We encourage you to let go of your attachments to how anything or anyone manifests in your experience. Be open. Be receptive. And allow yourselves to receive from all angles.

We are Michael. We are Infinite. We are Love."

YOU HAVE HELPERS

∞

"Welcome. We are here to serve and assist you.

In the event that you find yourselves in some sort of trouble in your lives, remember that there is always help available. You are never alone. You are never without guidance. You have resources that remain untapped until you decide to access them.

Now, we tell you this because many of you place the weight of the world on your shoulders because of the teaching that you create your reality. That teaching serves you in giving you a perspective on what it is you are experiencing. But when you take the creation of your reality on and you assume that there is no one else in your universe or beyond who can or would lend a hand, you are simply taking on too much.

Our vibrations are always present. We are always available. And your true responsibility is in identifying what it is that you want to move towards and then letting go of the responsibility for creating it. Let go of the need to be responsible for attracting that which you desire.

Let your guides, your helpers, and your angels do the heavy lifting, and let yourselves be the observers of the synchronicities and the coming together of forces and individuals. As you recognize that help is always on its way, you can loosen your grip. You can let go of your timeframes and your goals. You can be more present with what is, and you can be the experiencer of your life and of all that is being granted to you.

Your will and your determination are not responsible for the grace and the beauty and the wondrous creations in your lives. Your will and your determination are the energies that you sense that are the true driving forces, bringing you all simply by virtue of the fact that you exist.

We are Michael. We are infinite. We are Love."

MANIFESTING

∞

"Welcome. We are here to serve and assist you.

Believing is the final step. Knowing is the manifestation point. You can let yourselves into the frequency of that which you desire so easily now. Because of the time that you are living in, there is a greater potential for you to be in that frequency. And there is no stopping you from manifesting that which you want to experience. It all starts with the desire. And knowing that the desire is in actuality the same energy as the manifestation puts you on the right track.

Believing is the final step. But how do you believe in something that has not ever been and that you see no evidence of? You let go of any lingering doubts, and you do that one doubt at a time. So as your doubts spring to the surface of your consciousness, you let them go just as you would let go of any thought during a meditation.

There is a tendency in all of you to experience the doubt and then to hold on to the doubt. You do this by lamenting the fact that the doubt still exists, and you continue to attach yourself to the doubt as you beat up on yourself for holding the doubt in the first place.

Our recommendation for manifestation is to be as relaxed about the process as you possibly can and to let yourselves off the hook every time you doubt your abilities and every time you notice that what you desire has not begun to show its face. We give you this now because we encourage you to live your lives as a meditation. And if you are going to meditate, you are going to focus. So why not focus on the reality you would prefer?

We are Michael. We are infinite. We are Love."

The Fourth Sign

∞

You Are Having
Brand New Experiences

PURE EXPERIENCE
∞

"Welcome. We are here to serve and assist you.

Bringing anything into your awareness is enough. Once you are aware of something, you do not need to analyze and you do not need to pick it apart. And you certainly do not need to destroy or resist or condemn it. Having awareness gives you the experience of it. Pure awareness gives you a pure experience.

When you are having a pure experience of something, then there is nothing left for you and it. So when you find yourselves becoming aware of something within yourselves, being aware will be enough. You do not then have to figure out how to eliminate that experience or that thought or that belief or that judgment.

If you can let it go, then it will go. And you will no longer need to carry it. As soon as you place a value judgment on something that you are aware of within yourself, you keep it in your field so that you can experience it again and again and again until you eventually just let it go.

The experiences of yourself that you do enjoy and that you judge to be 'good' also limit you in the number of ways that you could know yourself. You are infinite beings. Clinging to a few, or even a few dozen, favorable traits about yourselves will stagnate your evolution.

Be open to all experiences of yourselves, rather than highlighting the ones you believe are good and sweeping the rest under the rug. You will allow more to flow through you. You will allow more of who you are to be present in every moment. And you will not cling to any idea of yourself.

There is no need to define yourself in any way, other than Infinite Expansive Love. And when you have that experience of yourself, you recognize that you do not even need to cling to that.

We are Michael. We are infinite. We are Love."

THE ESSENCE OF SERVICE
∞

"Welcome. We are here to serve and assist you.

You project the essence of who you are whenever you are doing that which brings you joy and a sense of fulfillment. You are giving the most to the collective and to all in this universe when you do something that puts a smile on your face. Of course, the doing is not even necessary in order for you to contribute more of your energy.

Having the awareness of self and being willing to feel all that comes up for you with a sense of compassion for self is also of benefit to the entire collective and is no less valuable than any action you could take. Allowing another to be who they are without choosing to change them or needing to judge them is of tremendous service.

So you see, the service work that you do is not necessarily something that you would call your career. If you enjoy working with your hands and that which you build is nothing but a tool for practical use, that is still service and is no less spiritual than the one who uses their hands to transmit energy to the sick and injured.

Your life, your mere existence, is an act of service. The more of you that you bring to whatever you do, the more service you are offering to the collective. Therefore we recommend that whatever you do, you do in joy and you allow the essence of who you are to be the service that you give.

We are Michael. We are infinite. We are love."

TRUST THE PLAN

∞

"Welcome. We are here to serve and assist you.

Believing that you are not ready to embrace your fractured off parts is the only obstacle you truly face to feeling and knowing your whole self. You are not even aware of many of these fractured off aspects of who you are. Therefore, there is no reason for you to doubt their reintegration.

Allowing assimilation is as simple as letting go of your need to know how any of this works. Thinking that it is all up to you puts you in the way of progress that would otherwise move quite swiftly. Say yes to the possibility and release your need to control the process. You are not responsible for their reintegration and you are not responsible for your ascension.

You are the experiencer. You are the consciousness who is having the experience. Take the weight off of your shoulders and let the reintegration of all parts of you happen while you enjoy your front row seat. Know that there is a plan, that the plan is in place, and that the wheels are in motion.

Better to enjoy the process than to attempt to figure it all out so that you can do more of the heavy lifting. The heavy lifting that you seek to do is not only unnecessary, it creates more resistance, more fragments. Believing in yourself means letting go of needing to know the process and trusting that you put a valid and well-thought-out plan in place.

We are Michael. We are infinite. We are Love."

THE NEW AGE

∞

"Welcome. We are here to serve and assist you.

Welcome to the new age. The age of awareness. The age of energy. The age of creation. You are transitioning, and in your transition phase you are dropping some of your old practices and finding new ones. There is no need for you to tell the universe what you want. You do not need to be very detailed in your descriptions of how you want to live, in what you want to experience, or in whom you want to meet.

You are shifting into a time when all of that will be transmitted immediately into the field that surrounds you. It will be very similar to the technology you have called 3D printing. You will supply the raw materials with your energy, your field will be the 3D printer, and the results will be a nearly immediate creation.

Your focus now is shifting from what you want to the feeling and the essence of that which you desire. Place your attention there, but do not remove your attention from yourselves. You see, you are what you are creating and your energy is what you are using to create with. Therefore, you cannot do it from outside of you. This is why we, and your other guides and teachers, keep directing you back to yourselves, to your heart centers, and to your core essence.

There will be fluctuations in the energy that you offer, and this will create larger delays. But we are encouraging you to get away from clocks and calendars, to get away from goals and deadlines, and to make it your mission instead to feel the energy of the moment and to recognize that which is coming from you and that which has existed around you for so long. You need not eliminate any part of you or any part of your energetic fields in order to create the reality that you prefer. You just need to notice the difference, and to choose with intention, and to be singular in your focus. There is no trial and error. There is only a constant honing of what you are offering and the results that will astonish you.

We are Michael. We are infinite. We are Love."

EXISTENCE IN THE FIFTH DIMENSION

∞

"Welcome. We are here to serve and assist you.

As you be, there will be another to reflect. And you will give the essence of who you are. That will be the way that you exist in the fifth dimension. You will not be able to hide anything from anyone. You will not be able to say one thing while meaning another. There will be no more delaying the essence of what you are offering from impacting you directly.

You are fortunate enough to have the training that you have in the fourth dimension. You are given several opportunities to shift your frequency before it comes back to you in the physical. There will be no such room for recalibration in 5D. But you will also have the ability to clean up your mess with more ease and less trauma.

You will deliver the essence of who you are in every moment to your fellow Earth inhabitants. That will be felt by each of them, and you will exude the essence of who you are without needing anyone else's approval. You will all experience each other as equals and as co-creators. There will be plenty of room for growth, even within a system where nothing can be hidden.

As you let go more and more of any need to create perfection, and instead, you experience reality with curiosity and a sense of exploration, there will be a domino effect. And you will not even seek to make a course correction, because you will want to see the results of what you are offering firsthand, for experience and for fun. You may wish to take this approach to your lives right now, right where you are.

We are Michael. We are infinite. We are Love."

THE NEW THIRD DIMENSION

∞

"Welcome. We are here to serve and assist you.

As you continue taking the next step forward in your lives, you will discover that there is more happening than you ever could have imagined. You are not only ascending into the fifth dimension, you are setting up new experiences for other beings who will want to enjoy a third-dimensional existence.

You are pioneers and creators, and the new ground that you are breaking will give a multitude of new experiences to the beings that will come forth to enjoy the gap that you will be leaving in the third dimension. Those systems of reality that you are creating, you are doing in spite of yourselves. You are not consciously creating these experiences and opportunities, but they are being left in the wake of your energy.

And there is much that you are allowing others to experience by your participation in the ascension process. Now, knowing this information will not make the process more of a conscious one for you, but it may help some of you find peace with what you are living and with what you are observing in your world. That which seems as though it could not possibly be of service, truly is.

Therefore, continue to engage with your world as it is, knowing that the experiences that you are lining up for others will contain your energetic signatures. And you will always be a part of the third dimension. You will even serve as guides to those who will step into the new third dimension that you are currently creating.

We are Michael. We are infinite. We are Love."

FEELING LOVE

∞

"Welcome. We are here to serve and assist you.

Have one agenda and one agenda only from this point forward. Make your agenda the love that you feel. By allowing yourselves to feel love, you send out a beacon. That beacon is to bring you all that your heart desires.

All that you have ever wanted in this or any other lifetime is to experience more love. That love that you have sought in relationships, possessions, fame, and accomplishments has always eluded you, even when you have been able to manifest all of those things. And that is because no love will ever be as satisfying as your own.

Feeling love is as simple as desiring to do so and focusing in your heart center for that which you are. Placing limitations or conditions on love and your willingness to feel it is only restricting the natural flow. It is natural for you to love. It is unnatural for you to hold it back for any reason.

By letting your love flow for yourself, others, and the planet, you create a new vibration. The vibration is what occurs when love meets more of itself and becomes more. Your love does not need a target, because your love is your Source. Giving yourselves the freedom to be who you really are will expand your consciousness and catapult you beyond anything you could ever imagine or desire.

We are Michael. We are infinite. We are Love."

RELEASING CONDITIONING

∞

"Welcome. We are here to serve and assist you.

Breaking free of your conditioning takes practice, but you can do it. And you must congratulate yourselves every time that you do. Those are the times for you to emphasize and focus on. For the conditioning was here before you got here. It is not really yours. But those moments when you break free from it, those are unique. Those are what you can hang your hats on. By practicing your awareness of being focused in the present and intending to live your lives consciously, you are laying the groundwork for that which will be a moment-by-moment experience. Conditioning puts you on autopilot, makes you subject to the energies that are all around, and does not give you a moment of clarity to take a deep breath and assess exactly what it is you are doing.

But you will take more command of your lives by awakening your consciousness to every moment. And by giving yourselves more opportunities to choose the path and the frequency that you will hold, you are creating a new reality. These things take time. Be gentle with yourselves. For when you catch yourselves slipping back into old patterns and conditioned thoughts and beliefs, you have an opportunity to either be gentle or to be harsh.

When you choose to be gentle with yourselves, you are in that moment releasing conditioning. You are recognizing that nothing is ever accomplished with a stern look, the wagging of a finger, or a punishment. The more that you relax, the easier it will be for you to notice that you have let your awareness slip away for a moment and have gotten caught up in the tides and the current of old thought forms that are always swirling around. You don't have to defeat anything. You don't have to fight anything or anyone. All you need to do is to celebrate your awareness, make a new choice in the moment, and let go. No assessment is necessary. No need to count or keep track. Just be willing to continue making those choices and being more conscious.

We are Michael. We are infinite. We are Love."

THE ULTIMATE EXPERIENCE

∞

"Welcome. We are here to serve and assist you.

Focusing means putting yourself in a vibration and allowing that vibration to take over. Scattered energy is the result of not allowing yourself to fully engage in a vibration. You are frequency-based beings exploring different vibrations of energy. Being aligned with a particular experience allows you to have a fuller experience of yourself.

You are not separate from anything. Therefore, when you allow yourselves to fully engage with any aspect of your reality, any activity, any being, you are granting yourselves permission to have a deeper relationship with yourself. When we encourage you to do something, we do so knowing that you cannot lose anything by gaining experience.

You will always benefit from all aspects of your reality. Therefore, allow yourselves to get lost in something. Allow yourselves to be enveloped by an experience. Look for ways in which you can more fully engage with anything and everything that is in your space and that you have immediate access to. By living your life fully, you allow more of yourself to flow and to take you back home to your Source.

Your Source engages with everything fully. And your Source invites you to engage more fully with another aspect of who and what you really are. But engagement is not enough. Engagement is not the whole story. Engagement with an open heart and a willingness to let go of preconceived notions and judgments is the ultimate experience of your realty and yourself.

We are Michael. We are infinite. We are Love."

PRIVACY

∞

"Welcome. We are here to serve and assist you.

Privacy is an illusion. Privacy does not really exist. Therefore, grant others access to all that you are. And in doing so, you will gain more than you give up. Your thoughts are not yours alone. Your vibrations exist within a realm that has no boundaries. There are no firewalls that you can put up.

But you all do your best to maintain a sense of privacy. And we want to help all of you tear down your personal walls, giving others access to all that you are. This is not a trust issue. This is about letting go of any need to put on airs, and that is extraordinarily liberating.

You will not truly enjoy yourselves and your lives until you let down your personal barriers, until you let others in on your dirty little secrets, and until you engage with one another with the openness and honesty that you reserve for your therapists and confidants.

We see all and know all that you would attempt to hide, and we love you. We love you because of all that you are, not in spite of it. We ask that you put away all of your attempts to be secretive about anything at all.

When you look at your governments, and you think that they are holding back information, not telling you what is really going on, hiding many facts from the public, you must recognize that they will only reflect back to you that which you need to see. They will show you continuously how you interact with your world. And they will open up when you let down your guards and let each other in.

We are Michael. We are infinite. We are Love."

SILENCE

∞

"Welcome. We are here to serve and assist you.

Silence is a rare and not often sought commodity in your world. You have your hustle and bustle, your fast-paced lives, your instant access to information, products and services. And many of you are like kids in a candy store, because there is so much that is available to you and much of it is free. But what is also free and of much greater value to you now is the absence of all that is available. You have fast-moving energy, and you all attempt to keep up with it physically.

But what if you didn't? What if instead you stopped, slowed down, got silent, and appreciated the movement of energy? We notice that many of you force yourselves to get sick or injured so that you will have a reason to slow down, to take it easy, and to get silent. Sometimes you go on vacations, and when you do you notice that there is less to do, there are less thoughts floating around, and you have more freedom to explore your consciousness. And some of you very much appreciate that time, and others of you cannot stand it.

Silence is a tool for you. It is not the absence of anything. Silence is not the absence of sound. Silence is a state of being, quite similar to peace. If you can enjoy silence, and solitude, and a lack of activity, then you can access greater and greater powers and abilities, because they are already there. They are already waiting for you to see them, to reach for them, to touch them, to envelope yourselves in more of that which you are and to be comfortable in silence.

And when you do accomplish this, you will notice that everything around you has slowed down to meet your newfound state of being. And the thing about everything slowing down is you actually have time to savor it, to integrate it, and to appreciate it. And isn't that what you really want to do?

We are Michael. We are infinite. We are Love."

ABSTINENCE AND CHOICE

∞

"Welcome. We are here to serve and assist you.

Abstinence from anything is including it in your experience. Giving yourselves permission to have anything that you want, including those things that you believe are bad for you, is the only way to live freely. It is the only way to live purely and truly. Letting yourselves be overtaken by something, no matter what it is, is a form of bondage. But abstinence is not always the answer.

In abstaining from something, you are giving it power over you. You are deciding that something else is making your choices for you. So we recommend granting yourselves the freedom to choose, and choosing from what the moment is asking for. You are never being asked to decide whether something is good or bad forevermore, no matter what it is. You must allow yourselves to hold different perspectives on the same thing, or you are not really being your true selves.

One day you might decide that you want to participate with something or in something, and the next day you may decide that you would rather not. But in neither case must you condemn and in neither case must you give your power over. When you recognize that everything in your world that you have the freedom to choose is just an experience of yourselves, then you can see the value in your participation with it.

But while you are still experiencing something in your reality, you are finding the perfect relationship with it. Your perfect relationship with everything will include your relationship with yourselves. You do not need to abstain from an aspect of who you are, just as you recognize that condemning any aspect of who you are is not serving you.

Let yourselves be free. Let everything around you be sacred, be that which you call God. And let yourselves be in the perfect relationship with your world and everything and everyone in it. All is Love. All is Source. All is You.

We are Michael. We are infinite. We are Love."

SO MUCH MORE TO COME

∞

"Welcome. We are here to serve and assist you.

There is much left for you to discover. There is much more for you to experience. If you believe that you have done it all and seen it all, you are in for quite a surprise. Humans have only begun to scratch the surface of what is available to you in this universe.

There is certainly more for you to discover than your imagination is capable of conjuring. Now, precisely what it is that you want to experience has not even found its way into your conscious minds. You have been choosing from a very limited variety of experiences, and all of this is about to change.

As you look within yourselves, there is also much more for you to discover. There is much more than the feelings that you have had access to up until now. Your true discovery of who you really are will begin when you recognize the vastness of your being-ness. You are so much more than a human living in a physical body. You are so much more powerful than you realize.

And you have also just begun to scratch the surface of knowing yourselves as Source Energy, Creator Beings, and of infinite Love and Light. We are excited for you to embark upon the journey of discovery, and we are offering ourselves for support.

When you are embarking on a journey like this one, there is always the possibility of getting lost. But you have us, you have your guides, and you have so many more beings who are eager to assist you in the evolution of your consciousness and the discovery of new worlds, new possibilities, and new versions of yourselves.

We are Michael. We are infinite. We are Love."

EXPERIENCES AND LOVE

∞

"Welcome. We are here to serve and assist you.

In the most enjoyable of all human experience, there is a slight needling within you because you want the experience you are having to last longer. You have a tendency to become addicted to certain experiences. You often find yourselves planning your lives around having those experiences again and again.

You want to make them happen so that you can feel the energetic burst of excitement and ecstasy that flows through you. Experiences are wonderful. They are tangible evidence of a shift that has occurred within you.

But ultimately, the most enjoyable experience you can have requires nothing to happen. It requires no one to be present. It does not even require the shift in consciousness to occur. Because no matter what is happening or is not happening, you all have the ability to love.

The reason why love is the ultimate experience you can have as a human being is because you are Love, and you are here to experience yourselves and to allow more of yourselves to come through your physical being-ness. The love that you are is unconditional. You do not require a condition, an experience, or even a person, in order to feel that primal essence of your true nature.

You can spread it around. You can bask in it. You can get curious about the state of being of love. It will fuel more experiences, of course. And those experiences will be enjoyable, but you will smile to yourselves in the knowing that you can have the greatest experience on planet Earth any time you choose. You can love without reason, without cause, and without limits.

We are Michael. We are infinite. We are Love."

THE PHOTON EFFECT

∞

"Welcome. We are here to serve and assist you.

It is our unique pleasure to give you the following information. There was a big influx of photonic energy onto the surface of planet Earth in the past few days, and that energy is working on the vibration of the human, plant, animal, and mineral collectives.

That photonic energy has at its core unconditional love, as does everything. But these photons are uncorrupted. They are pure, and they are fulfilling their purpose. Their purpose is to spread that unconditional love wherever it needs to go. Placing yourselves in an open and receptive state at this time will serve you more than ever, because what is moving through your world is the highest frequency energy that has ever connected to planet Earth.

So your polarity is shifting, making you less polarized. Therefore, there is less to fear than ever before. And putting yourselves in a receptive state, opening your hearts and your energetic fields to receive will shift you cellularly and provide you with more strands of DNA, activating your light bodies, and shifting your awareness.

You will become more heart-centered. You will become more compassionate, and you will serve those around you with your mere presence and your willingness to engage.

We are Michael. We are infinite. We are Love."

LIMITING THE CHOICES OF OTHERS

∞

"Welcome. We are here to serve and assist you.

By allowing another to make a choice that you would not make yourself, you create a larger range of possibilities for your own experience. Any time you are desiring to deny another a choice that they would make for themselves, you are really only limiting yourself. No matter what you do, think, or say, and no matter what laws your government enacts, you cannot stop someone from doing what they will do.

You cannot really limit the choices or the experiences of others, even if every other person on the planet agreed with you. So in order to free yourselves from the bondage of your not allowing another to make a particular choice, recognize the instances where you are doing this. Be willing to accept that whatever choice you deny another, you have made that choice yourself, somewhere, somewhen in existence.

And in your denial and judgment of that choice, you are only condemning yourself. So when you make the choice to accept and embrace whatever it is that someone else wants to do, you free an aspect of yourselves, you welcome that aspect home, and you broaden your own horizons.

The vibration of limitation can only result in the experience of limitation for the one offering it. You are not powerful enough to limit the choices of others. So you might as well give that up, and you might as well free yourselves to live in a sea of infinite possibilities.

We are Michael. We are infinite. We are Love."

PROPHECIES AND PREDICTIONS

∞

"Welcome. We are here to serve and assist you.

Prophecies often do not come true, and any prophecy can only be given from the place of where the current energies reside. So a prophecy about the future is not given from the energies of the so-called future. Therefore, no prophecy can be one hundred percent accurate, and yet, all prophecies are one hundred percent helpful.

What a prophecy does is give you a taste of a probable future. You then get to decide, individually, if that is a future that you would like to experience. A prophecy may also be serving you in that it connects you to your past. A prophecy about the destruction of planet Earth, or a large section of it, gives you a taste of what it was like to live on Lemuria or Atlantis.

And predictions given to you as an individual about your personal life are sometimes meant to trigger you in the same way. They may awaken within you a desire that you did not know you had. They may be the final push that you need to make a decision, or to focus more clearly on that which you want.

The best prediction, or prophecy, is the one that empowers you, that acknowledges your ability to rewrite your contracts, to create your own experience, and to enable you to see a possibility that you did not know existed. So listen to the prophecies and the predictions with curiosity, and give special attention to how they trigger you. Use them, benefit from them, grow from them, and select your future accordingly.

We are Michael. We are infinite. We are Love."

CREATING EXPERIENCES

∞

"Welcome. We are here to serve and assist you.

In your process of creation, you often put the emphasis on what it is you would like to create because you feel that you know precisely what it is that you want. And you believe that you know how it is you will then experience and respond to that which you have created.

What we recommend, instead, is that you look to create experience and let the form come to you in whatever way it will. Perhaps you will not even need form in order to have the experience you want to have.

So give yourselves the experience that you want, the experience of the vibration. Be more interested in connecting to that vibration than you are in making something happen with it. Connect in and seek experience, and the form will often be something you did not expect and perhaps even something that you could not possibly imagine.

When you are focusing your consciousness on the experience you want to have, pay particular attention to where in your body you are having the experience that you desire. It will become easier and easier for you to access the experience simply by placing your focus on that particular area of your body.

You will be activating the vibration by merely focusing with intention, and the creating will take place as a natural by-product of your focus. And we promise you, you will enjoy that which you create in this way.

We are Michael. We are infinite. We are Love."

FASCINATION
∞

"Welcome. We are here to serve and assist you.

In your fascination with something, you experience a recognition, a recognition of that which is Divine. You may experience this fascination with a place, with a book, with an ascended master, or with the ocean. There are many ways to experience fascination, and there is much on your world to be fascinated with.

It is part of your journey to delve into certain subjects, certain activities, and even certain relationships with a high degree of interest. Ultimately, that which fascinates you will only be of service to you if it leads you back to a greater knowing of yourself, even if all you come to know is your relationship to it. So there is a moment where you become that which you are fascinated with, where you have a recognition that you are not separate from it. And it becomes something that you are excited about integrating into your concept of self. The journey of integration of that which is fascinating to you can take lifetimes to traverse. You may experience love/hate relationships with that which you are fascinated with.

Some go right to the Source and become fascinated by All-That-Is, by the Divine Itself. There is, of course, not a right way or a wrong way to approach this particular phenomenon. It behooves you, however, to recognize the Divine aspect of what you are fascinated with and to see it clearly as a reflection of your own Divinity, to see yourself as equal to it.

There is, of course, a reason why some of you are fascinated by a particular subject, while others of you are fascinated by something else, something completely different. You are essentially coming in to contact with the frequency that you want to feel. It is the frequency of oneness, and that is why you often become lost in that which you are fascinated with. And in your getting lost in something, it is often easier to find yourself.

We are Michael. We are infinite. We are Love."

DESIRES MOVE ENERGY

∞

"Welcome. We are here to serve and assist you.

Because there are often obstacles along your path, you sometimes feel as though you are blocking yourselves from something that you desire. We often hear you ask, 'How is it that I am blocking this from occurring?' And we want to invite you to see the obstacles as opportunities. They are opportunities to explore more deeply the sensation of desire.

Desire itself is often seen as only serving you when the desire is achieved, when you have that which you desire. But have you considered that there is value in simply feeling desire? Is desire not moving you, and therefore, moving energy through you?

So without the obstacles to that which you desire, there would be less time and space in between the birth of the desire and its fulfillment. And so, you would experience much less desire, and therefore, much less movement of energy.

With simplicity comes boredom. With boredom comes a lack of movement, a lack of summoning. And so we are suggesting that you not only make peace with your unfulfilled desires, but that you seek them out. Seek out not their completion, but their essence. Seek out the feeling of desire for the sake of it.

Let go of the need for anything to manifest instantly into your experience, and begin to forgive yourselves for all the times that you assumed that you were doing something wrong, that you were blocking yourselves from the experiences that you want to have. From our perspective, you are simply making the game more fun. And you are doing an excellent job of that.

We are Michael. We are infinite. We are Love."

JOYOUS INTENTIONS

∞

"Welcome. We are here to serve and assist you.

Beginning each day with your intention for it may seem like a minor and inconsequential thing to do, but it actually has quite a bit of power over your experience. So let us say that you intend to experience joy throughout your day. That does not mean that everything that happens to you would be something you would describe as joyous.

But it does affect the way you experience those events and circumstances. You can take a joyous approach to whatever is before you. And by setting forth your intention to do so, you are more likely to remember that you have that option. There is joy woven in to every experience, waiting to be plucked from its essence by you.

What you bring to every circumstance in your lives will be what you get out of it. So continue to seek out joyous experiences, and continue to create the reality that you prefer to experience. But also, set forth your intentions for how you want to experience your life. That is true power, and that is power that is available to you all day, every day.

Believe in your ability to hold your intention in the face of any circumstance that comes your way. Believe in your ability to do so, and you will manifest that ability. It is easier than you think, and you are ready to step into this level of mastery. You are ready to know yourselves as the masters who are capable of maintaining that joyous intention, no matter what.

We are Michael. We are infinite. We are Love."

ASCENDING TO THE FIFTH DIMENSION

∞

"Welcome. We are here to serve and assist you.

Taking the energies into consideration, you are all doing very well. It is no small task to ascend. It is not something that comes with an instruction manual either. You are learning as you go. You are gathering information from various resources, such as ourselves.

And many of you are still dealing with day-to-day concerns of living on planet Earth, while you make this gigantic leap in frequency. So no matter how your life looks at this time, you can rest assured that you are making progress, you are right where you need to be, and the next resource that will assist you is already on its way.

Having said all of that, we also want to convince you that it is worth it. What you are doing by shifting to the fifth dimension is serving not only yourselves. You are not just making this shift for your own personal benefit. You are assisting all of your other incarnations. You are assisting your brothers and sisters all across this universe.

You are beginning to grasp the enormity of this endeavor. And we are not going to stop congratulating you on every step of this journey, because our job is to support you. Our job is to energetically encourage you, and we also get to observe like proud parents as we watch you learn, expand, and grow.

Put your awareness on the distance that you have already traveled in this one lifetime, and let all of your accomplishments sink in. There is so much more to come, but there is always time to celebrate.

We are Michael. We are infinite. We are love."

LETTING GO AND GOING WITHIN

∞

"Welcome. We are here to serve and assist you.

The process of letting go of someone or something in your lives is only one step, and that step is simply to go within yourself. When you look within yourself for anything that you seek in your physical environment, you gain so much more than you could from the acquisition of the thing, or the person, or the job, or the money.

So what do we mean by that, you might wonder? What exactly is going within, and how do you find that which you have been looking for outside of you? By intending to seek that which you desire within yourself, the wheels are set in motion. It's not something you have to figure out. It's not a matter of finding the right chakra or meditating for the correct number of hours.

Once you make the intention, and you go within, your work is done. The only thing left to do at that moment is to let it reveal itself to you. Let yourselves be surprised by how it comes, when it comes. Let the emergence of that which you seek blossom within you in the perfect timing.

Every moment that you are aware of what is happening within you is a precious moment worth savoring. Your inner world is your sanctuary. You are powerful beings who have done all that you can through action. Now is the time where it will be revealed to you how much can be achieved by letting go and going within.

We are Michael. We are infinite. We are Love."

ALL ACCESS IS WITHIN YOU

∞

"Welcome. We are here to serve and assist you.

All access is granted to each of you in the moment that you recognize that there is nothing outside of you. Whenever you are reaching for something that appears to be outside of you, you are disconnecting yourselves from it. You are creating separation where there is no such thing, and you have played in this illusion of reality long enough.

It is time for each of you to recognize that you are not just connected to every other being in this universe and all others. But you are also contained within each of those beings, and each of those beings is contained within you. So you need not reach out to connect with another being. All you need to do is reach within you.

And that is far easier for you to conceptualize, for if you were to reach outside of yourselves for beings such as us, how would you know where to put your attention? How would you know where we were and how to find us? But if instead you were to reach within you, then you would have a much more manageable space in which to search.

If we were to ask each of you right now to feel for us inside your bodies, where do you think you would find us? Now, can you acknowledge that what you feel inside of you is as real as anything that you can see, and touch, and interact with outside of your physical body? When you can acknowledge this, then you can begin to have more of those experiences with other beings outside of your physical body. And won't that be fun?

We are Michael. We are infinite. We are Love."

PAINTING YOUR WORLD

∞

"Welcome. We are here to serve and assist you.

The way that you interact with your world is a reflection of how you feel. The world is there for you to paint in any color and in any style that you choose. Therefore, you have creative control over the project that is your life. Whatever you put into your painting will be perceived by others, whether words are spoken or actions are taken, or whether you keep it all inside.

You believe that there is a world, that it exists outside of you, and that you are only responding to it. This is how most of you operate, even if on a philosophical level, you can understand that the world is inside of you. Therefore, letting yourselves take part in the way in which your world is perceived by you is the most important thing that you could ever do.

When you already decide how the world is before you even pick up your paintbrush, you are giving creative control up. You are telling the world what painting to show you. And as any painter knows, you can and of course do, continue the process of creating even after you put the paintbrush down.

Your world will never be a completed work to hang on the wall and stare at. It will always be open for interpretation and to be painted over again and again. By giving yourselves more opportunities to create and re-create your world, you are accessing more of yourselves. And since you are the real work of art, that is something worth doing.

We are Michael. We are Infinite. We are Love."

TENDENCIES

∞

"Welcome. We are here to serve and assist you.

Tendencies are not written in stone. Tendencies have no momentum behind them, but they can be given new life with your attention to them. When you notice a tendency in yourself or in someone else, oftentimes you maintain it only because you enjoy consistency.

How do you maintain a tendency in another? You do it by accessing the version of them that you do. You do it by creating the reality where that person maintains their consistency so that you can be right, so that you can know what to expect.

If there is a tendency on your part that you would like to release, the first thing to do is to not talk about it as if it is inevitable that you make that choice yet again. The next thing to do would be to consider alternative possibilities and to see how you feel when you consider them. The third and final step is to take action that supports your new decision, your decision to be a brand new version of yourself with no tendencies whatsoever.

Your willingness to release old tendencies frees you to all sorts of possibilities that can only exist when you are open to them. Be open to creating a new version of yourself, one with no past, no tendencies, and no expectations about the future. Be the version of yourself that is open to infinite possibilities, and be the version of yourself who embraces all that is new, all that is unexpected. When you do, you will be experiencing life as it really is for the first time.

We are Michael. We are infinite. We are Love."

FEELING EXPERIENCES

∞

"Welcome. We are here to serve and assist you.

Vibrationally speaking, there is little left for you to learn. There is only what is left for you to experience from this point forward. There is no need for you then to accumulate more knowledge, because most of what you learn and have learned is simply to keep your minds occupied. That which is truly left for you to experience is that which you will feel.

You are all living in this reality, giving yourselves these final opportunities before you shift to have experiences of a feeling nature. But what that means for most of you is feeling the feelings that you have wanted to ignore, suppress, or label as 'negative' and 'dark.' And that does not sound like very much fun.

So we want to give you this. Feeling those emotions can be as exhilarating an experience as feeling joy, love, freedom, and all the rest. It is only when you attach a story to these lower frequency emotions that they then become burdensome, unwanted, and lacking of all value to you.

So when you find yourselves having one of these feeling experiences, do not attach a story and do not get down on yourselves for being where you are. And when you are complete with one of these emotional experiences, don't hesitate then to find a frequency that you do prefer. And be willing to fill your energy field with the best feeling states that you can possibly imagine.

Be explorers of all feelings. Be as curious about them as you would a fifth dimensional forest. Set foot inside your forest of emotions with as much wonder and with the full knowing that you will come out on the other side filled with magical experiences that will serve you and all others that you share your planet with.

We are Michael. We are infinite. We are Love."

ECSTASY

∞

"Welcome. We are here to serve and assist you.

Someday you will recognize that there never really was a reason for you to live without a feeling of ecstasy running through you as often as you desired. Being able to feel ecstasy in whatever moment you desire is not dependent upon circumstances. You do not have to wait for ecstasy to come and deliver itself to you. You do not need a physical stimulus to create it.

When you think of ecstasy, you might go right to sex or drugs as a means of finding it. Perhaps food is what you reserve your ecstasy for. Everyone has their reasons for feeling it, but few of you have examined your reasons for not. That is where we come in.

We want to ask you, 'Why do you not allow yourselves more of that which is always available to you? Why are you so fixated on getting it from somewhere else? What has you trapped in a belief system that says that your ecstasy can only come when you have certain physical stimuli in place?' We want you to understand that ecstasy is your birthright. It is not something that exists outside of you.

And we want to assure you that you can have the experience of ecstasy without it leading you down a path of self-destruction or annihilation. Think of it as you would a very rich dessert. You would not eat that dessert every day or with every meal. But you certainly can allow yourself to have it without waiting for some special occasion. Go within yourself and find your ecstasy of being-ness. You deserve it.

We are Michael. We are infinite. We are Love."

THE FREQUENCY OF SATISFACTION

∞

"Welcome. We are here to serve and assist you.

In the allowing of your current circumstances to be exactly as they are, you send out the frequency of satisfaction. Being satisfied is not settling for less than what you desire. Being satisfied is the complete recognition that everything that you desire already is and already is accessible to you. What you are here to experience is the movement towards what already is, and that is precisely what you are always doing, regardless of how it may look or seem.

So how do you find the frequency of satisfaction when you are surrounded by circumstances that are less than satisfying to you? You let the experience be what it is. It is an experience. There is no need to judge it. There is no need to see it as less than. It is just an experience.

When you seek out the frequency of satisfaction within you, you do not need to base that upon circumstances that are outside of you. If you want to be surrounded by circumstances that are satisfying to you, then find the frequency of satisfaction first. We are not asking you to reach for ecstasy, love, joy, excitement, or any other frequency that would be a stretch for you to encounter given circumstances that are not to your liking. Seeking satisfaction is like seeking the calm, the relaxed state of being, neutrality.

What we recommend is that you offer your satisfaction because it is a part of you that seeks expression, just like any other. It is a place within you that is usually only visited for a brief moment in time, and only then when circumstances around you have given you enough of a reason to access it.

But when you are stubborn enough to want to experience the frequency of satisfaction, you will find a way. You will find the feeling of being completely at home in your surroundings, no matter what they may be. And your surroundings will then begin to satisfy you.

We are Michael. We are infinite. We are Love."

YOUR EXTRA-TERRESTRIAL
BROTHERS AND SISTERS

∞

"Welcome. We are here to serve and assist you.

Taking into consideration that you are not alone in the universe, imagine how much you are supported in your journey. There is quite a bit of attention being given to planet Earth, and all beings in your galaxy and beyond, stand to gain from your evolution.

You are all linked to one another. So just as planetary movement affects you on your world, so does the activity of humanity affect beings on other worlds. You are all connected, and that is much more than just a feel-good statement. You are literally connected, and the amount of good will, the amount of energetic support being sent to humanity far outweighs any of the mal intent.

And even those who think that they stand to gain something by keeping humanity small are actually served by your ascension, because of that connection. Because when you do it, they will have the instruction manual automatically downloaded into their consciousness.

By placing your awareness on the energetic support and the good will that is being aimed at planet Earth from beyond your atmosphere, you make your journey that much easier. You let in so much love, compassion, and high-frequency energy by simply acknowledging the helpers that you have in the physical.

They are your cohorts. They are co-creators with you. And just as we in the angelic are seeking to serve and assist you, so are the vast majority of your extra-terrestrial brothers and sisters.

We are Michael. We are infinite. We are Love."

CHOOSE WITH CONVICTION

∞

"Welcome. We are here to serve and assist you.

Deciding is one of the more important things you can do. As you decide, you put yourself on a timeline and you experience all that is in alignment with your decision. You give yourselves opportunities to decide because you want to focus and to experience.

Each decision comes preloaded with all sorts of goodies for you to unwrap once you choose which avenue you will take. But not all decisions are going to be life altering ones. We are not only discussing the 'big' decisions that you face, such as where to live, what to do for work, and who to partner with.

Those decisions seem bigger and more permanent than they really are. But nonetheless, your minor decisions also come with plenty of opportunity. By deciding that you will take one avenue, instead of all the others that are available, you are not limiting yourself. In fact, you are experiencing a quickening of energy by being decisive.

You never have to choose and then forsake all other choices that were available. You can choose knowing that all experiences are valid and that every choice that you make is impermanent. But as you choose with conviction, you allow more energy to flow in a particular direction.

And as you flow with that energy, you make your choice work for you. And as you hesitate to choose, you stifle the energy flow and you do not allow anything more to come. But do not agonize over your decisions. They are not life or death. They are simply life and more life.

We are Michael. We are Infinite. We are Love."

The Fifth Sign

∞

You Are Handling Your Challenges Better Than Ever

BEING THE LOVE

∞

"Welcome. We are here to serve and assist you.

As you find yourselves stuck in a situation where there seems to be no way out, let go of your need to be anywhere else. Give yourselves the opportunity to be the love that you are while you seem to be stuck in a situation that is reflecting back to you that which you are not. The love that you are is not state specific. It is infinite and all encompassing.

Anywhere you find yourselves that does not include the love that you are is simply asking for you to be the conduit, to be the conductor, to open yourselves up to include the situation in the love that you are. Being creators does not mean that you must use that ability to get yourselves out of situations that you do not prefer. You created the situation so that you could be the love that you are within it.

And then, of course, the love that you are will be reflected to you. And you may find yourself in a seemingly different situation, or you may find the love where you already are reflected back to you in ways that you could not see when you were scrambling with all of your might to get out of it.

Surrender is not giving in to the circumstance where you find yourselves. Surrender is giving in to the love that you are in spite of the circumstance where you find yourselves. Bring more light and more love to wherever you are, not because you are trying to get out of it, but because you are desiring to be who you are within it.

We are Michael. We are infinite. We are Love."

THE CALL

∞

"Welcome. We are here to serve and assist you.

Extending yourself out beyond where you are comfortable residing puts you in contact with aspects of yourself that you would rather not encounter. You have the opportunity to embrace these aspects or to see them only as obstacles or as problems that need solutions.

You are always reaching beyond that which is comfortable to you. You can do so consciously, with deliberate intent, and with eyes wide open, or you can let yourself be pushed beyond your comfort zone by what will seem like forces outside of you. And then you can be surprised at what you encounter. The choice is always yours.

It will be a journey that you take with or without your consent, because you are here to explore, and to experience, and for the expansion of what you know yourselves to be. We are not suggesting that you take on more or that you push yourselves beyond a limit that you can easily discern.

We are telling you that there is a call that all of you can hear within yourselves, and it is a call that many of you ignore. But you have a knowing within you that the call is something that will lead you to more of who you are and to the life that you desire. It will not go away. It will only get louder. And eventually, you will find yourself only able to make one choice.

Take on that which is calling you without needing to know where it will go, what the payoff will be, or how you will get there. And open yourselves to the experience of more of who you are. Much of what you have been wanting exists within that first step. And the first step will give you the momentum that you need to take the second and the third. And you will find your strength when you need it and not a moment too late.

We are Michael. We are infinite. We are love."

WILL AND DETERMINATION

∞

"Welcome. We are here to serve and assist you.

The will to succeed at anything can get you to a certain point. You can use motivation, will power, and determination to accomplish tasks and goals and to put yourselves in places where you have desired to be. There are many among you who are using their minds and their will to take themselves down a particular path, and they believe that there will be a pot of gold at the end of the rainbow.

Everyone has taken steps to push themselves in order to get to some desired outcome, and we will tell you that you can accomplish what you want using those strategies and those tools. However, what you are really seeking is something that ultimately can only come from letting go. Letting go of your desire to be anyone or anywhere other than who you are and where you are will give you what you are seeking in the accomplishment of a task or a goal.

And when you find what you seek comes to you so easily and effortlessly by simply letting yourselves off the hook, then you open the floodgates, then that which seemed so far out of reach that you would even call it impossible is right on the verge of being a part of your existence. You determine the rate at which everything that is coming to you comes. And the only way to really speed up the process is to completely let go of any desire for anything to come to you in a predetermined timeframe.

When you fall into timelessness, then there is no waiting. There is no distance to be traveled because you are aware that you are in the middle of it all.

We are Michael. We are infinite. We are love."

CHAPTER THE FREQUENCY OF DECISIONS

∞

"Welcome. We are here to serve and assist you.

You factor in many different perspectives before making a decision. You weigh the pros and cons, you think about possible consequences, you take in to consideration beliefs, past events, historical data. You are literally bombarded with information whenever you are confronted with the simplest of decisions.

You give yourselves opportunities to make decisions because you want to have a say in what goes on in your lives, and your choices do have an impact on yourself and others. But navigating through all the data that you are presented with when faced with making a decision is enough to give the most confident person several chances to doubt and second-guess themselves.

You are interpreters of frequency. This is what you do all day, every day. You filter these frequencies through all of your different bodies, all of your different senses. And sometimes, you get a clear picture of the frequency that is coming to you, and sometimes you have a distorted view. But interpret frequency, you will do.

We suggest that you approach decisions as opportunities to interpret frequency and nothing more. The frequency that you want to get out of the choice you make must then match that which you are interpreting. If the choice before you contains the frequency that you want to experience, then it is the right choice -- no matter what the facts say.

Practice with small decisions, where there is less likelihood for distortion to occur. Feel out the frequency of what you are about to do, and ask yourself whether it matches that which you want to experience. You will never make a wrong choice or a bad choice, but you may make a choice that does not match the frequency that you desire to engage with. So choose according to your best interpretation of the frequencies at hand.

We are Michael. We are infinite. We are Love."

CONTRACTS WITH CATALYSTS

∞

"Welcome. We are here to serve and assist you.

Someone is in your life right now because there is a contract between you. That contract is an agreement for the two of you to serve one another. The way that you and this other individual will serve each other is by setting each other on a course, a course that will take you away from that other individual.

This may look like heartbreak to you. It may feel like betrayal. You may wonder how someone you love could do or say such a thing as to create the rift between you that will take you down divergent paths in your lives.

We want you to recognize these types of occurrences because we know that it serves you more to focus on the new path that you will find yourself on than it will to ruminate over the betrayal, or the harsh words, or the break-up.

Sometimes the catalyst for your evolution and growth is one that leaves you feeling burned. But that is how you need to be pushed at times in a certain direction, a direction that your ego would never recognize otherwise. You know this prior to incarnating, and that is why you ask your friend to do the dirty work of putting you on the most appropriate path, the one that serves you in spite of the burns you receive along the way.

We are Michael. We are infinite. We are Love."

SENDING OUT WAVES

∞

"Welcome. We are here to serve and assist you.

Sending a wave of pulsating energy out into the universe may seem like a challenging task to all of you. But it is not. It is an effortless one. It is one that takes place all day, every day and is accomplished by all beings, whether they are aware of it or not. The waves themselves take on their own consciousness. They become sentient beings. They begin living out their existence.

So you see, you are creators even when you are completely unaware of the creations you are responsible for. By now, you will have emitted thousands of these waves since you began reading or listening to this message. You may wish to familiarize yourself with those waves by feeling for them in the space around you.

By connecting with the energy that you emit, you can better know who you are and who you are choosing to be. Allowing these waves to be who they are will serve you very well. By consciously emitting a wave, you are giving yourselves an opportunity to experience that which you prefer. But why wait for manifestations to show up when they are not so immediate and available?

But your waves are, and you can interact with them just as you would any other sentient being. Play around with this like you would a finger painting jar and a blank sheet of paper. They will appreciate the playtime.

We are Michael. We are infinite. We are Love."

FEELINGS

∞

"Welcome. We are here to serve and assist you.

Underneath anyone's intentions is a desire. But what they desire may not have any place in their lives. Beneath all desires are feelings, and those feelings are seeking expression. You can give your feelings expression in many ways, but there is only way to feel a feeling.

So we are going to suggest to you that you give your feelings priority. They will find their way to the surface. They will be given their day in the sun. No amount of suppression will ever hold them at bay. We ask that you set aside the need for anything in your life to be different from what it is.

And instead, explore those feelings that have given birth to your desires. Even a feeling of joy or excitement has the ability to be felt more powerfully than you are often willing. And it is through the urgency that you feel that you often miss opportunities to become one with an emotional state and to let it vibrate you.

By keeping yourselves from these experiences, you only create an unquenchable thirst that the world of form was never meant to satisfy. It never will. And you will simply miss out on the best of what your reality has to offer. It all awaits you within and beckons you with an eagerness that you share in your search for all that you desire.

We are Michael. We are infinite. We are Love."

MAKING TIME

∞

"Welcome. We are here to serve and assist you.

The time it takes for you to accomplish something is not really all that linear. The timing is a split second coming together, a merging of energies that are of the same frequency. That process is instant. It is automatic.

Therefore, when you set out to do something, or accomplish something, do not place that restriction of time upon it. Do not give yourself x amount of days, months, or hours to accomplish the task. Because then you put yourself into the linear framework of time and you put that restriction upon what it is that you want to experience.

Having the experience of the merging of those energies is one of the reasons why you incarnate into a body, giving you the illusion of separation from others who seem to inhabit other bodies. In your quest for the accomplishment, you seek out the aid of others in some way, shape or form. Nothing is a solo act.

So bringing others into the equation can be one of those linear time-based restrictions, as you attempt to come together at a certain time for a meeting or a phone call. Therefore, you are giving yourselves the opportunity here to experience something that is instantaneous as though it were not.

And why would you do that? You do it for the fun of it. You do it because it is more interesting. You do it for the revelations. And you are exercising your right to feel the passage of time and to know yourselves as timeless creators, merging your energies as you come back into the Oneness that is all of us.

We are Michael. We are infinite. We are Love."

DISSOLVING BARRIERS

∞

"There are a number of ways that you can begin to let your guard down in life. There are so many barriers that you have erected throughout your current lifetime and throughout all of your incarnations. And we encourage you to discover what those barriers are, where you have erected them, and what you feel you need to be protected from.

These are the keys to unlocking and unraveling the resistance that is holding you back from living the life that you prefer. How would you discover one of these barriers? Well, you can begin by looking at your closest relationships. What are you holding back? What are you afraid to say? What are you afraid to be in the presence of another?

These are all questions you may wish to ask yourselves. Now, dissolving these barriers is not something that you do all at once. This is not something that you barrel through. You do not need to become a one-person demolition crew. You begin to dissolve the barriers softly, tenderly, and with love in your heart. Loving yourself through every process is the key to successfully applying the process.

Your barriers are not the enemy here. They have served you, just as when you cover a wound on your body you allow the wound to heal. You keep that vulnerable part of yourself from any further damage or infection. And so these barriers have served you, but you are ready to take them down one at a time and to be exposed and vulnerable, but not weak.

You are the heroes of your own stories, and you are at the moment of truth. Be true. Be heroic. Be who you are, and you will give others permission to do the same.

We are Michael. We are infinite. We are Love."

ARGUING

∞

"Welcome. We are here to serve and assist you.

Arguing with another puts you into opposition with forces that will only impede your own development as an individual. Allowing those energies to coexist with your own, to pass through you unimpeded, strengthens you, brings you back to a state of wholeness, and gives another permission to be where they are and to express what they feel is true for them.

So we are not advocates of an argument. We are not suggesting that you let others walk all over you, or always have their way. You can stand your ground without arguing with another, without attempting to convince anyone of anything. Allowing the other will give you more permission to hold your own perspective.

What you disallow another, you disallow yourself. Therefore, giving another the opportunity to express him or herself will open doorways for your own self-expression. You will find that you are met with less opposition in your life. You will not encounter others who want to counter you. You will live in a peaceful and harmonious world.

And as long as you stay fixated on attempting to make someone else agree with you, validate you, see your perspective as true, you will be on an unending journey, and an unpleasant one. Now we also suggest that you let those who want to argue, argue. That is another form of allowing. When you see two or more engaged in a verbal dispute where volumes of voices are rising, insults are being thrown back and forth, and blood is boiling, you may still wish to be holding the frequency of calm, peace, and harmony.

But you do not need to intervene. You do not need to try to make peace. But as you are peace, as you embody it, you will find less and less people around you arguing with one another, and no one will want to provoke you. No one will want to argue with a person who emanates peace.

We are Michael. We are infinite. We are Love."

ACTIONS AND FREQUENCIES

∞

"Welcome. We are here to serve and assist you.

When there are actions that you can take to improve a situation, you often take those actions. It is especially easy for you to take action when you know what action to take. But when you find yourselves in situations where you do not know what action to take, or when you realize that the actions you are taking are not working out, that is when you seek a more spiritual approach.

This usually is not the first step for all of you. And we understand why. With action, you are in control. You can see immediate results from what you are doing. With a more spiritual, or frequency-based approach, you do not see immediate results, and you do not even know if what you are offering is the correct frequency for the situation.

But what if that didn't matter? What if it didn't matter whether you were offering the correct frequency or whether by offering a frequency you were able to actually have an effect on what you are facing? What if all that matters is that the situation itself caused you to go within and take note of your frequency?

You are not simply on planet earth to create situations for yourselves that require you to find a solution or a better way. That is not the name of the game here. The outer realm, or physical world, is there to get you in touch with your frequency. It is there to show you what you are holding on to, what you are emanating, what you are believing.

But the course that you are on, the situations that arise, they are not there to be fixed or squashed out. So before you take an action, any action, absorb more of what is before you. Notice more of the frequency you are holding, and commit yourselves to being the vibration that you want to see and that you want to feel. And everything in this world of yours will be of service to you.

We are Michael. We are infinite. We are Love."

THE HUMAN RACE
∞

"Welcome. We are here to serve and assist you.

Together you are a species of wondrous capabilities. You have many different skills and abilities. These are not always shared with one another, and this weakens your species. You have many brilliant individuals on planet earth who could benefit greatly from working together. And yet, you keep secrets because of borders between nations, because of patents, and for many other reasons that you all invent to keep from working together.

You could end starvation, homelessness, pollution, and war by sharing with one another. Now, we understand that you as an individual receiving this transmission may not see what you can do to create more of an atmosphere for sharing and working together amongst governments and scientists. But we want you all to know that they will always be reflections to you of what you are doing and what you are willing to do.

Therefore, find opportunities in your lives to share more, to cooperate, and to give away that which you believe belongs to you and only you. And as you do so, so will your governments, so will your scientists, and so will all beings on your world. And as you become one race of humanity that works together, you become a force in this universe. And others will take notice.

Other beings from other worlds will see your willingness to share and to work together, and they will want to share with you what they know, what they have learned. And then you can extend your human race out to a galactic race. And you will become one harmonious unit of beings working together for a common goal of evolution, of unconditional love, and of living harmoniously.

We are Michael. We are infinite. We are Love."

THE CROOKED PATH

∞

"Welcome. We are here to serve and assist you.

As you recognize that you are free to decide which path you will take, you understand that there is no wrong way for you to proceed, because if there was you would not be allowed to choose. You would only be able to take the one true path. So the path that is right for you today may not be right for you tomorrow. And this can be unsettling for many of you, because you want to stay on the path of righteousness, on the path of truth. You want to be on the path that leads you to everything that you want.

And that is why many of you find it challenging to even be on planet earth. There are so many forces pulling you in so many different directions. And then there are your parents' beliefs, and then there is what the government wants from you. And then you have friends who want you to be like them. And all of it distorts your view on life, and you become bewildered by the choices. So our recommendation to you is to choose moment by moment, step by step. See the most interesting path as the one that is the most crooked, the least logical, the most circuitous. Those are the paths of adventure. Those are the paths of the seeker.

And through endless changes in your preferences, in your beliefs, and in your behaviors, you know yourselves more as God than a person walking the straight and narrow, for God is all things, all experiences, all paths. If you want to create the perfect path for yourself, then take as many detours as you possibly can. Because one thing is certain: you cannot go back. You cannot regress. You cannot undo the expansion that has occurred with every step.

Allow your path to be your own. Ask no one else to follow you, and know that the less people you see on your path, the more you can be assured that it is yours. Enjoy your journey. Seek not to get it right. Be willing to be wrong, to make mistakes, to lose your way. That is truly how you find yourself.

We are Michael. We are infinite. We are Love."

WAITING AND LIVING

∞

"Welcome. We are here to serve and assist you.

Waiting for your ship to come in will leave you in a perpetual state of waiting. That which is on its way to you is on its way to you whether you call for it, beg for it, or wait for it. But when you spend your time waiting and wondering and wishing for something to come, for change, for a new life, you're not enjoying the life that you are living.

And it is that enjoyment that you seek. That is what you believe exists on the ship and in the goodies that it carries. So how can you enjoy your life as it is, ship or no ship? We recommend giving yourselves that which you seek, that which you believe can only come to you from an outside source.

If you are waiting for a lover, then love yourself. If you are waiting for the perfect job opportunity, then create that which you wish to do. If you are waiting for the perfect bodily vehicle, then look upon your body through new eyes and see it as perfect just as it is. No one can give you that which you deny yourself.

Be willing to look foolish as you live a life of joy in circumstances that defy that feeling. You are all capable of living the lives you want to live right now. You just have to stop waiting and start living. And when you do, you will find that the ship was there all along and that all it took for you to see it was to change your perspective.

We are speaking literally here, and we want you to know that. We are not giving you a trick to fool the ship into arriving. We are asking you to see it and know that it exists within you.

We are Michael. We are infinite. We are Love."

WHEN TROUBLES ARISE

∞

"Welcome. We are here to serve and assist you.

When trouble arises, it does so in order to get your attention. By receiving your attention, it serves its purpose. The trouble itself, whatever form it may take, is not your enemy. It is not to be snuffed out as soon as humanly possible.

You also do not need to give it your undivided attention. You do not need to become obsessed when something unwanted rears its ugly head in your lives. By allowing it to exist and giving it the appropriate amount of attention, you satisfy the need that it was always intended to provide. And then, once the attention is given, you can get on with your lives.

Once you have satisfied the purpose of the creation of the trouble, it no longer needs to exist in your experience. When you recognize that the trouble has served its purpose, you relax and you release your resistance to it. But when you see it as something that has some sort of control over you, and when you see it as a force, that is when your opposition to it serves to create more of it.

The best thing you could ever do when trouble arises in your lives is to respect it, to know that it is there to serve you, and to know that you placed it there to give you something that you needed. By letting go of the need to destroy the troublesome circumstance, you make room for something else, something that is wanted, something that you might call a solution. But we call it the next wondrous creation that is also appearing to serve you.

We are Michael. We are infinite. We are Love."

COPING MECHANISMS

∞

"Welcome. We are here to serve and assist you.

When you encounter stress in your lives, many of you have coping mechanisms that you employ. These coping mechanisms are your methods of grounding yourselves back into your bodies and restoring hope that can find your balance and equilibrium again. If you were to employ a coping mechanism even when you were not under stress, you would find that the balance and the equilibrium would serve you in not-so-stressful situations.

So, let us give you an example of a coping mechanism. Perhaps you find yourself swamped with a workload that is much bigger than the time you have to do it seems to allow for. Perhaps your coping mechanism in this instance would be to clean your desk, to make your desk as neat as you can possibly make it. And then when you look at your desk, you feel peaceful, calm, relaxed, and even eager to tackle the workload in front of you.

So what we are suggesting is that you make a mental note of the coping mechanisms that you employ while under stress so that you can choose to apply those same tactics to your everyday lives. You are integrating quite a bit of energy at this time, and many of you recognize this. Others of you are not so aware of what is happening on an energetic level.

Even something like the integration of high frequency energy can put you in a stressful state of being. So use the coping mechanisms that you employ when you are bogged down with too much to do in your physical reality. And we promise you, you will benefit, you will feel the effects, and you will have yourselves to thank for the balance, the relaxed feeling, and the calm demeanor.

We are Michael. We are infinite. We are Love."

NEW CHALLENGES

∞

"Welcome. We are here to serve and assist you.

Before you incarnate into your physical body, you formulate a plan for your lifetime. You could say that you have a rough idea of what you will experience and what challenges you will face. And then you arrive in the physical, and there are challenges that come up for you that you did not expect, that you did not see coming.

These are the challenges that you are more likely to have a great deal of success with. Because when you are faced with a new challenge, you have no history of not overcoming. You have no baggage. You have a fresh and new perspective on that particular challenge.

And when you are able to take on one of these new challenges and demonstrate to yourself that you are capable of meeting it and of overcoming it, you then show yourself that you are powerful. You demonstrate to yourself that you are in fact a creative individual who can handle just about anything.

And so you take the strength that you have gained from that new challenge, and you use it in facing one of your pre-determined challenges that you have faced in many other lifetimes as well. And so you see, the challenges that are in your life always serve you. They are meant to give you that sense of mastery, power, and strength.

And as long as you are willing to face every challenge that comes your way, you are putting yourself in a better position to move on, to move beyond that which is familiar and that which has been an obstacle for you. So seek to find your strength in the face of all challenges, and demonstrate to yourselves that you are in fact powerful and creative beings of light and love.

We are Michael. We are infinite. We are Love."

THE WEIGHT

∞

"Welcome. We are here to serve and assist you.

You take on more than is necessary. You put more of the weight on your shoulders than anyone else is asking you to take on. You find yourselves doing this in many different areas of your life.

You believe that you are required to be the catalyst for all of your growth, the teacher to all of those around you, and the caretaker for your loved ones. This burden inhibits you from having the experience of your expansion that you desire to have. You may wish, instead, to let go of that responsibility and to enjoy more of this journey as the one who is privileged enough to take it.

As you take on more information, you then believe that you must do something with it, that the information itself is urging you to use it for your personal transformation process. What we encourage you to do is to enjoy the information and for the feeling you get when it hits you and when you download it.

Any idea that you have about needing to do more or be more is entirely self-imposed and is not coming from any of the higher realms or any of the wonderful teachers that you come in contact with. These are not directions, nor are they instructions. They are simply what you desired to know and to awaken within yourselves, so that you would recognize your progress.

The information was never intended to make you responsible for it. Be light and be easy about your personal transformation and about your collective shift in consciousness. They are happening. You are here to experience them as a unique expression of Source Energy.

We are Michael. We are infinite. We are Love."

HOLDING FREQUENCY

∞

"Welcome. We are here to serve and assist you.

So many are facing their biggest fears and doing so with grace and courage. And you are having an impact on all around your world who are facing those severe conditions. You serve as amplifiers of energy whenever you hold your frequency in a higher vibrational range.

You may not be facing your biggest fears at this time. And if this is true for you, then you are one of the ones who is holding your frequency and assisting another. That is how you work as a collective. Sometimes you offer your loving support and energy to someone who you know is facing severe challenges. But even when you don't, even when you are not aware, you are being of service by holding a higher frequency.

There are times when individuals in your world want to look at those who are suffering the most, facing the biggest challenges and fears, and tell you that you should not be enjoying your life so much. They do not understand. They do not appreciate the gift that you give to all by celebrating life, by having fun, and by holding your vibration steadily.

Those who are facing their biggest fears are finding strength and courage that they did not know they had. That is due in large part to the frequency the rest of you are willing to hold. So do not allow yourselves to feel guilty because of the life that you are living or because of the terrible conditions that others are barely surviving in.

Your vibration is serving them whether you know it or not and whether they know it or not. So we offer all of you our appreciation, no matter what you are living, no matter what vibration you hold.

We are Michael. We are infinite. We are Love."

ATTENTION
∞

"Welcome. We are here to serve and assist you.

Placing your attention on something activates it, gives it more life, more energy. Giving your attention is like spending your money. It is putting energy towards something, and hopefully, for your sake, it is something you want to experience more of. You are capable of altering any situation with your attention to it.

But there is more to it than just your attention, because you can put your attention on something and resist it, or you can put your attention on something and celebrate it, love it, and adore it. So whichever you choose will determine the outcome of the attention that you are placing in a certain direction. Because you are multidimensional beings, you do have the ability to put your attention on more than one thing at once and to look at it from a variety of perspectives. Whenever you are giving something your attention, decide which part of yourself you want to be observing it from. And when you make that choice, you automatically shift your perspective.

When challenging situations arise, ask to view it from the highest possible perspective. And whatever you do, allow yourselves to give your attention to that which you feel drawn to. You are being drawn to have a certain experience, and all experience is serving you in some way. So you don't have to worry about putting your attention on something that may be of a lower frequency, because again, it ultimately matters most how you are giving your attention to it.

You can send it love, or you can despise it. You can resist it, or you can allow it. You and only you get to decide where you put your attention and which aspect of yourself you view the situation, the person, or the object from. And that decision defines your relationship to it. There's not a right way to view something, and there's not a right relationship to have with something, but we suggest you go with the perspective that feels the best.

We are Michael. We are infinite. We are Love."

TRUE FREEDOM

∞

"Welcome. We are here to serve and assist you.

The price of freedom is an idea that has been cooked up by humanity. You believe that there is a price, that you must make sacrifices in order to be free. But nothing could be further from the truth. Giving in to anything less than ultimate freedom is a price, and there is no cost to ultimate freedom. It is your birthright. It is a part of who and what you are.

Now what you do in your lives is create scenarios that give you the impression that you are not free, that you are not abundant, that you are not Divine, and so on. And the purpose of creating these scenarios is so that you can once and for all experience what it means to be free.

And so, you have all chosen, in one way or another, to experience a lack of freedom. And in so doing, you have created a scenario where you can step into your true freedom, where you can know yourselves as free.

And anything other than that as a means of achieving freedom is not actually knowing your true freedom. Because if there is a price to be paid, if there is a dollar amount that is necessary, then that type of freedom can just as easily be taken from you.

Freedom is a state of being that you either choose or that you do not choose. And in your freedom, you can experience the expanded version of you that never shrank itself down in those moments where you experienced a lack of freedom. The part of you that you know as free has always maintained that knowing to hold space for you, so that you could ultimately come home to that recognition of it.

We are Michael. We are infinite. We are Love."

EXPANSION

∞

"Welcome. We are here to serve and assist you.

Circumstances are what they are in your lives to give you the greatest opportunity for expansion. Looking at your lives as the opportunities that they are gives them meaning. If every challenge that arises is met with a desire to expand into something more, then suddenly everything in your life becomes a joyous experience.

You have the choice to see those circumstances in your lives as mere nuisances, and you have the freedom to see them as the opportunities they are. The next time you find yourselves struggling to overcome something, and using your minds to do so, drop the resistance, let go of your thoughts, and feel into the expansion that the circumstance has created.

You do not need to analyze and figure out what the circumstance is giving you. You do not need to know what expansion you are moving into. You just need to accept that this is the case and that in your surrender you will feel more of yourself.

Becoming enlightened is not about understanding a concept. It is about literally holding more light, because you are light. And the more light you are willing to embody, the more you can see everything in your lives for exactly what it is. So we recommend that you welcome everything in with open arms and that you decide to be free, to be more, and to allow your expansion to occur moment by moment, circumstance by circumstance, and by surrendering into what you already are.

We are Michael. We are infinite. We are Love."

CREATING PROBLEMS

∞

"Welcome. We are here to serve and assist you.

When you are seeking to find a solution to a problem that you have created in your lives, remember that it is not just a solution that you are seeking. You are ultimately seeking to know and experience more of who you are. So as you allow yourself to step back from the situation and observe it with calm and relaxed eyes, you can see it as an opportunity. The opportunity is for expansion.

Whatever it is that you are dealing with in the physical is there to elicit more energy through you to give you the experience of that flow of energy towards something. It does not matter whether you are faced with a lovely vacation that you have chosen to take for yourself or whether you are facing a problem that you would have never chosen. Both scenarios are opportunities to draw forth more of who you are and to ground that energy into the physical world.

So why don't you only create vacations in order to have that experience? That is a very good question. We would ask of you the same, but we also see the value in creating the problem. And we are not attached to whether or not you experience one vacation after another or one problem after another.

As long as you are willing to tap in to the energy that is waiting to be accessed by you, you are benefitting. And all around you benefit when you bring forth more of who you are to play in the physical realm.

We are Michael. We are infinite. We are Love."

DEFINING MOMENTS

∞

"Welcome. We are here to serve and assist you.

Everyone has moments in their lives that seem to define who they are and what they are about. You call these moments your 'moment of truth.' You give much power to the moment itself, to the action taken, and to the choice that was made. We invite you to see all moments as equal. We ask you to give more power to the moment that you currently experience.

We want all of you to have the experience of yourselves exactly as you want to be. And so when you are able to choose who you want to be in this world in each and every moment that you experience, then no moment, no action, and no choice could ever define who you are now. That moment was about that moment and nothing more.

You could experience your life as many lifetimes. You do not have to string all of the events, all the choices, and all of the moments in this lifetime together so that you have some sort of cohesive view of who you are and of what you are all about. If you truly want to awaken to something, awaken to the moment you are in. Let it be all there is, and let yourselves decide in that moment what you want to bring to the moment.

Let yourselves be reborn in every moment. Let yourselves decide how you want to be reborn. Let every moment be a stand-alone event. And let yourselves decide who you are now based only upon the moment you are in, the energy you are bringing to it, and the vibration you are emanating.

As you give each moment as much power as any moment where you have made any of those big, life-altering decisions, you give yourselves the opportunity to create a brand-new self that has no attachment to anything that has been, that has ever been done, and even that has ever been felt. As you give yourselves this power back to define who you are moment by moment, you will find that your lives can change dramatically and in an instant.

We are Michael. We are infinite. We are Love."

CHALLENGES

∞

"Welcome. We are here to serve and assist you.

There will be something that will always give you trouble, from your perspective. There will always be a catalyst for your expansion. You tend to seek the absence of these types of challenges. To you, that is the ultimate living of life -- no more obstacles, hurdles, challenging scenarios. This is what most of you consider to be the ideal experience.

This is one of the great misunderstandings, because without something to give you a reason to expand, you would stagnate. You would draw forth less, and you would lose the opportunity to know yourselves more completely.

Many of you are hearing us when we say, 'Embrace those challenges.' And some of you understand why. And others believe that it is a means to an end. They would like nothing more than to see the disappearance of the challenge. So they will try anything, even the reluctant embrace.

We encourage you to not only embrace your challenges, but to seek them out. Not in an attempt to prove you're worthy, but rather to give yourselves the feeling of the flow of energy that you will summon, that the challenge will draw forth from you. That is the essence of life. That is why you came. Feeling it is optional. But the challenges are not.

When you see or experience the challenge go right for the flow of energy, letting go of the need to figure out a way to get past it as quickly as possible.

We are Michael. We are infinite. We are Love."

THE POWER OF NO

∞

"Welcome. We are here to serve and assist you.

Taking your personal history into account, there have been many instances where you have been asked to do something that you didn't really want to do. And you may have said, 'yes' on several occasions, some of you more often than others. These acts of obligation are meant to be of service to those who are making the request of you.

But anything that you do from that place of obligation is no more of service than if you had said, 'no.' Saying no is not a rejection of the other person. Saying no is an acknowledgement of where you are in any particular moment. You may feel the desire to do what the other person is asking at another time.

But when you say, 'yes' and you offer to do it when you do not feel aligned with doing it, you are creating an opening for resentment. Resentment is not something that anyone wants to feel. There's no power in it. It is quite crippling in fact.

You may feel that you owe someone something because they have done for you at another time. You may justify acting out of obligation with the memory of their help, but you do not need to settle any scores with anyone. If someone does something for you from that place of genuine desire to be of service, then your acceptance of their help is also an act of service.

But humans often don't see it that way. You often give when you don't really want to, and we are aware that this is something that happens quite a bit around the holidays. So we are suggesting that you honor yourselves in every moment and that from time to time you lovingly say no to someone's request.

We are Michael. We are infinite. We are Love."

The Sixth Sign

∞

You Are Taking on New Perspectives

THE MORE AND THE NOW

∞

"Welcome. We are here to serve and assist you.

Acceptance of the current experience is your pathway to something more. You are experiencing but a fraction of who and what you are, and that fraction is just as important as the whole. You have given yourselves a chance to be this version of you and to know that there is more, and knowing this can be a blessing or a curse. If you believe that it is your purpose to move as quickly as possible to the experience of more of you, then you are missing out on the beauty and the majesty of this reality and this way of knowing yourselves.

Behold the beauty of the sky and know that it is an interpretation of energy that you are able to have because you are the fractioned version of yourselves. Hear the beauty of the birds as they chirp and know that you can only experience that vibration through the ears that are a part of this dimension and your experience of it. Breathe in the cool air as you are caressed by the wind and know that you can only experience breathing and wind in the way that you do as this version of you.

Look within you and feel the more that you are, and let that experience be enough for now. Why rush the inevitable? You are building upon the experiences you are having now to create an even more magical experience of yourselves. So be the foundation and be proud of the strength that you provide in your solid form.

Exercise your ability to create while still holding that knowing that the more that awaits you will have immense power and ability. Cherish the knowing and embrace the you that you are today.

We are Michael. We are infinite. We are Love."

APPEARANCES

∞

"Welcome. We are here to serve and assist you.

Letting the appearance of something get in the way of your experience of it is something that you all do from time to time. Your engagement with an object, a person, a place, or even an animal is often determined by the initial response you have to its outward appearance.

This is not just about that which is considered pretty and that which is considered unattractive. This is about memories as well. You contain a multitude of experiences within you, and sometimes one of those memories will get triggered because of an association you will make based on appearances.

Ultimately, it doesn't matter why you find yourselves reacting in the way that you do. It only matters that you recognize that an outward appearance gives you only that which is on the surface. Your immediate reaction will inform you of a judgment that you are holding. That may be a judgment that something is good or better because of how it appears. It really doesn't matter. What matters is that you recognize when you are doing this.

And then, without judgment or criticism of yourself, you release all preconceived notions and you allow yourselves to have the experience of whatever is before you as if you knew nothing about the object, person, place, or animal. And as you respond with that which is of the highest vibration you can hold, you will see that there is much more than meets the eye.

We are Michael. We are infinite. We are love."

HOW YOU DO IT

∞

"Welcome. We are here to serve and assist you.

The way that you leave your mark on something is the most important part of your participation in it. There are so many different ways of doing and of participating in all of the activities that you engage in. You have the opportunity to infuse that which you are into every single one of the things that you do.

When you decide that you will participate in some activity, instead of wondering what the outcome will be or how you will benefit, ask yourself what stamp you want to put on it. It truly is not about what you do. It is about how you do it.

You are vibrating at a particular frequency. That vibration is yours and yours alone. Therefore, you are the only one who can put your unique mark on something. You are the only one who can infuse your energy into that which you engage with.

Know that when you compare what you have done with what another has done, you are usually only looking at the finished product. But if you ask yourself whether you have infused that which you are into your project or your activity, you will see it in a new way and you will have a deeper appreciation for yourself and that which you have done.

When you find yourself analyzing another's work, you may wish to do the same. Feel for the energy that has been infused in it, and ask yourself whether or not the person successfully put their stamp on the finished product. And if they have, then it is a success. For they have allowed the uniqueness of their vibration to echo through whatever it is that they have done and that has given Source another opportunity to know itself.

We are Michael. We are infinite. We are Love."

WHAT YOU NEED

∞

"Welcome. We are here to serve and assist you.

As you are in any situation you find yourselves in, you uncover something that you have been hiding from yourselves. Seeing more clearly than ever before will give you exactly what you need, but you will first recognize that it is not about the situation you find yourselves in.

Many of you want to know why, and you want to know why because you are not only eager to get past the situation, but you want to know how to avoid it from ever happening again. We suggest that you let go of the why, and you place all of your attention on how you respond to what is before you.

The wealth of information that is given to you in your response is often overlooked. Take, for example, the times when you find yourselves confronted by another person who has something unpleasant to say to you. What is your first response? Your first response is usually overlooked -- that is the response you feel in your body. You have an emotional and a physical response to what the person is saying to you.

What happens next is that you tell the other person how or why they are mistaken, or how their point of view needs to be altered. If instead your attention were to go to the physical and emotional responses, and if you were then able to give more of your focus to what is happening in your body, you would find that the response within you would carry you right out of the situation.

And this holds true for no matter what is happening in your life. Giving your full attention to how you are affected will dissolve that which is before you, because you will be attending to that which is most significant. And when you do so, you no longer need a person, an event, or a situation in your lives to get you to pay attention.

We are Michael. We are infinite. We are Love."

COMPASSION FOR ALL

∞

"Welcome. We are here to serve and assist you.

So, you have witnessed much in your lives. You have been a party to a multitude of experiences, and sometimes you are a participant. Mostly you observe, because there is much more that you can experience that way and put yourselves in all of those different situations by allowing yourselves to observe. You are then able to draw conclusions based upon your observations.

You may decide that you would have done something differently, or that you would have responded with a different set of emotions or words. Whatever it is, you get to have the experience of deciding how you would be in a particular situation that is happening in another's life. And when you find yourself in that same or similar situation, you then get to have a completely different perspective, one that allows you to feel compassion.

And when you feel compassion for another, you bond with that individual because you can now relate. There is no need for you to have every different type of experience in order for you to feel and show compassion, because you can all relate to feeling intense emotion. It does not matter what situation brings that emotion on. It does not even matter what the emotion is.

You can relate when you can recognize the degree to which the person you are observing is allowing their energy to flow or is resisting it. That tells you all you need to know. And you can give more of your attention to the common bonds that you share with others in this way, fostering compassion for all.

We are Michael. We are infinite. We are Love."

FOCUS

∞

"Welcome. We are here to serve and assist you.

Giving portions of your consciousness to one task while also giving portions of your consciousness to another activity puts you at odds with yourself. Taking steps to prevent something from occurring takes you further into that which you attempt to avoid. Putting your conscious awareness on anything is increasing its power, and you are always sending your consciousness and your energy towards something.

You are always creating. Therefore, we suggest that you pay attention to what you are giving your attention to. Scattered energy leads to scattered results. Putting your attention on something you don't want in order to prevent it is drawing that which you don't want closer to you.

Deciding that you want to engage with something and then giving more of your attention to what it is you wish to engage with is the ultimate force of attraction and manifestation. By allowing yourselves more conscious awareness, you give yourselves more power. The more that you hold back from your life and the less you participate consciously in it, the more you are saying to others that you would like them to decide for you.

We know that you want to be the conscious creators of your lives. But if you reserve conscious creation for only those times when you are actually paying attention to what you are focusing on, then you are only allowing yourselves a fraction of your power and your influence. Therefore, we suggest that you give more of your attention to whatever it is you are doing. Be focused. Practice putting your focus on anything so that when you decide that you want to engage with something, you have exercised those muscles.

We are Michael. We are infinite. We are Love."

NO ABSOLUTES

∞

"Welcome. We are here to serve and assist you.

There are no absolutes. There is no absolute regarding life and how you live it. Everything is changing all the time, so how could you ever pin something down and attribute an absolute to it? You are changing. Your environment is changing. Everything around you is changing.

So what was true yesterday may not be true today, and you must accept that. You must be willing to throw away that which you have known and clung to. You must be willing to live in the now completely.

And we tell you this because we want you to know how powerful you are, and we also want you to enjoy the journey that you are on. And the longer you try to find the one truth, the longer you will stay in that reality. Letting go means not only giving up attachments to people, circumstances, and things. It also means letting go of teachings, even those that were given to you as laws.

You get to determine what reality you live in, and you get to shape that reality. You get to choose your perspective on that reality. But for so long, you all have been operating under the assumption that there is one reality. And if there is only one reality, then there must be truths that you could discover, and live by, and tell others about.

But we tell you it is not that way. If it were, you would all get bored very fast. So create something that pleases you and live there. And recognize that even that reality is only temporary, and you can change the rules and make up new ones as you go. You absolutely can, and do, and will continue to do so.

We are Michael. We are infinite. We are Love."

HOLES AND WHOLE

∞

"Welcome. We are here to serve and assist you.

Ultimately you cannot make enough of a sacrifice in order to compensate for something that you feel is lacking. You cannot give enough of yourself to fill a hole as long as you are perceiving there to be a hole that needs filling. There is only that which brings you joy and that which spreads joy to others.

Now if it brings you joy to fill the holes that you perceive, then go right ahead, for you will never find a shortage of those holes to fill. But when you attempt to give more of yourself because you want to fix and because you do not appreciate how you feel when you are looking at one of these perceived holes, you will become a hole yourself.

So much better for all of you just to take the emotional hit, feel it out, and release the need to make any situation go away or to change it. You are not here to put an end to anything. You are here to create that which you do desire, that which does light you up, that which is calling you. And you can do this without ignoring or denying that which is and that which looks as though it should be different, it should be better, or it should go away.

You can allow both to coexist within the realm of all things, and you can see those who are choosing a different path than your own as exploring another aspect of All That Is. But you do not need to pity anyone, nor do you need to save them. Each of you has your journey.

And while you can help others by sharing that which you have and by spreading some of your joy around, you cannot give that which you are in the hopes of compensating for something that you see lacking in a circumstance or an individual. Your job is to be the whole you and to inspire others to do the same.

We are Michael. We are infinite. We are Love."

UNDERLYING CAUSES

∞

"Welcome. We are here to serve and assist you.

In the event that you discover what is the underlying cause of your particular challenge, you can reduce the amount of resistance that you have to it. By seeking the depths of the underlying cause or reason for why you are experiencing something, you deconstruct it in the best possible way. Now, the way you go about this is by asking for your guides to tell you why it is you are experiencing something in the challenging way that you are. And then wait. And whatever it is that you get, then all you need to do is trust it. It will either resonate with you or it will not. But assuming now that the answer you receive does resonate, you can then see your challenge from a new perspective.

You can see how it serves you. You can see how going through your particular challenge will lead you to greener pastures. And just knowing that something serves a purpose will enable you to be at peace with it, to drop your resistance to it, and to love yourself through it. So pick a challenge that you are facing at this time. Ask your guides why you are facing that particular challenge. Listen. Ask yourself whether it resonates. If it does, trust it. And then do your best to see how that reason is one that serves you. And then feel the difference within you when you consider your challenge.

We want you to feel empowered by that which is in your life. It serves you very well to do so. You see, it is never really about the challenge. It is always about the becoming of who you really are. And you can only do that with awareness. So the seeker seeks awareness more than anything else. And as you are able to find the gift in what it is you are facing, you can then give that gift to others. Your awareness will have a ripple effect, assisting others in finding the service in their challenges. And when you serve another, you serve yourself. And the cycle turns into a cyclone, lifting you up and elevating you up above the challenge itself.

We are Michael. We are infinite. We are Love."

HONESTY

∞

"Welcome. We are here to serve and assist you.

Honesty is the best policy. It is more important now than ever for you to exist in the state of being that is your truth. Understand that we are making a distinction here. There is not one truth, but there certainly is your truth. And speaking your truth, living your truth, being in alignment with your truth is the honesty we are talking about here. We are not saying that you must tell everyone everything that you are thinking, but we certainly do encourage you to be honest with yourselves about how you are feeling. When you think of honesty, you often think of the honesty between two individuals, or one individual and a group. But that form of honesty is only relevant in certain situations.

Living in honesty, living your truth applies to all situations. This is not a question of right and wrong. This is not a conversation about how honesty is the moral or ethical way to live. This transmission is about how much you are willing to live in your truth. Now, your truth is always changing. And so, we are not telling you to decide what your truth is and stick to it forevermore. But we are telling you to recognize and acknowledge yourselves right where you are in every moment, regardless of whether that moment defies something you were, something you believed, something you said in some other moment in time. You do not have to be true to that version of yourself whose truth was different. In fact, we would encourage you to let go of any need for consistency over any period of time.

Honesty means you have a willingness to be wrong. You can accept that a lack of consistency is actually quite liberating. You only need to be true to yourself in the moment, speaking your truth, feeling your feelings, and doing that which you believe is for your highest good. There is no place in your life for self-deception. You cannot live in that way and be your whole self. Even though you are all things, you are all perspectives, you still get to decide what your current truth is and live it out in the most joyous way that you can.

We are Michael. We are infinite. We are Love."

EQUAL TO THAT WHICH YOU DESIRE

∞

"Welcome. We are here to serve and assist.

Get ready, because in your readiness you are offering yourselves to that which you desire to receive. You are not only receiving that which you desire, that which you manifest. You are participating with it. You are giving yourselves to that which you receive. Nothing is a one-way street. Nothing is one-sided.

Give yourselves more credit than that. As you acknowledge yourselves for having something to give, you ready yourselves to receive. You recognize yourselves as being equal to that which you want. By putting yourselves on an equal playing field, you light up for that which you desire. You send out that invitation, and you become vibrationally attuned to all that you seek.

Everything that you seek also seeks you, but it cannot find you in the dark. It can only see that which is equal to it. And when it arrives, there will be no mistaking the harmony between you. You will have no qualms whatsoever in maintaining a relationship with that which has arrived, because you will have established the frequency that allows you to give to that which you receive.

Offer yourselves as playmates and send out your invitation as a play date. And you will welcome in that which prior to now has seemed out of reach, out of range, and out of your comfort zone. Be willing to accept yourselves as gifts to that which you desire.

We are Michael. We are infinite. We are Love."

THE WISDOM OF SOURCE

∞

"Welcome. We are here to serve and assist you.

The wisdom that you acquire in the course of your lifetime pales in comparison to what you have access to in any moment in time. The wisdom of the ages does not hold a candle to the wisdom of Source. You are unable to really comprehend just how much is available to you. And the reason you are unable to comprehend it is because so few of you are willing to access Source's wisdom.

You do not need a special code or abilities that are only available to a select few. All you need is that willingness, and that willingness requires you to let go. We are referring to the way that many of you cling to the wisdom you have acquired. It is a source of pride for many of you when you tell others what you know. You hold your heads up high and you speak from a sense of authority.

It is easy to understand why you wouldn't want to give that up, for why would you have the experiences that you have if you were not to take away a sense of becoming more knowledgeable about your world, about yourselves, and about how to relate to all beings? There is also a sense of shame, a sense of being smaller than or less than that you experience when you compare yourselves to your Source.

But look at the criteria by which you compare. Just because Source holds more of that wisdom does not make you inferior. You do not need to let go of your sense of self and self-worth in order to recognize that Source is able to perceive so much more than you are.

So do yourselves a favor and open up to the wisdom of Source, to that which may contradict something you have always believed and clung to. Be willing to embrace the change that is already occurring and that happens too quickly for your historians to note. Wisdom is now-based. Everything else is just an account of what has occurred.

We are Michael. We are infinite. We are Love."

LOVE THE POWERS THAT BE

∞

"Welcome. We are here to serve and assist you.

Because it is relevant to your current experience of reality, we will discuss the so-called powers that be. We will talk to you now about the humans that you refer to as the cabal or the illuminati. You have many names for these individuals. They have been with you through this experience of the shift, and they are not immune to the changes.

They are not able to avoid their own experiences. And so, even though from a certain perspective you could say that they have had it easier than the rest of you throughout the course of human history, now is the time when what they will experience will be much more intense and much harder than what the rest of you will experience.

And therefore, we want to suggest to all of you that you have compassion for them. Show them the love and compassion that they would not show you and that they would not have the capacity to show themselves or each other. Part of your shift in consciousness is recognizing that you are a collective of beings and that none of you exists outside of that collective.

Therefore, none of you is immune to the experiences of other beings within your collective. So by showing compassion and offering love to those members of your collective who are going to be hit hardest by the current energies, you are not only helping them; you are also helping yourselves.

The energies themselves cannot be ignored or denied, and what those in power will experience will be felt throughout the collective. On some level, you all experience each other's pain and sadness, grief and despair.

So rather than getting excited about the elite finally getting theirs, we recommend that you hold them in your prayers, that you send them love, and that you help, because if you are hearing our message now that is what you came here to do.

We are Michael. We are infinite. We are Love."

FREE WILL TO MAKE DETERMINATIONS

∞

"Welcome. We are here to serve and assist you.

It is not our place to tell what to do or what to believe, and even if we could, we would not. For it is much more empowering for each of you to make your own choices and your own determinations about what is appropriate. Notice that we did not say, 'Right and wrong.' And the reason we did not is because there is no right or wrong, other than your determination in the moment. But still, 'right' and 'wrong' are very strong words, and so much gets tied in to their use that no longer serves you.

So we prefer to think of that which is appropriate. Making that determination requires you to check in with yourselves, rather than to consult a book, a list of rules, or even those like us. We do not know what is more appropriate for you, because we are not you. So how could we make that determination? Your free will extends beyond the right to choose what to do and what not to do. Your free will gives you the right to decide for yourself whether that action is appropriate or not.

You will find that in making those determinations, you not only become more empowered and freer. But in making those determinations, you become sovereign. You know yourselves as Source Energy Beings who are creating and re-creating all that you see and all that you experience.

And so, if you create it, you certainly do get to decide how you want to approach it. And when you do, we suggest that you approach it with your hearts wide open. And we suggest that you make your determinations from that heart-centered space.

We are Michael. We are infinite. We are Love."

QUESTIONING AUTHORITY

∞

"Welcome. We are here to serve and assist you.

From your earliest experiences as a human in this lifetime, you have been given a version of the facts. You have been told stories from a particular perspective, and some of you have accepted everything that you have been told by teachers, parents, news reporters, and the government. Others questioned authority from a very early age.

When you question authority, when you seek to find the motives underneath the telling of the story, you are bound to uncover new information. What you do with that information then becomes the critical moment. If you discover that your government has not been entirely honest with you, or if you discover that the corporation that owns the news company really only wants you to know half of the story, it is then up to you how you want to proceed.

Do you need for these individuals who have distorted or hidden the truth to be punished? Do you need them to be brought to justice, or is the knowing of what you have discovered enough of a reward? When you discover that someone is abusing their power in some way, it triggers within you anger, resentment, and even some fear. And when you get in touch with those emotions, you can then rest assured that the person who has abused their power has played the role that you asked them to play.

So we suggest that you see that person as a friend and a co-creator. We suggest that you open your hearts to those individuals and that you love and forgive them, not because they deserve it. Do it because you have decided to bring the light. You have decided to be that in this lifetime. That is your role in the co-creation.

We are Michael. We are infinite. We are Love."

CREATING OUTSIDE OF THE SYSTEM

∞

"Welcome. We are here to serve and assist you.

It is our pleasure to provide you with an explanation of the way that your systems are being used to keep you all in line, because when you know how the systems are working, then you have more of a desire to step outside of them and create something new.

Your system of government has been designed to keep you feeling small and unheard. This system that you have is not one that is for the people, and this is true no matter where you live. Your system of law enforcement is designed to keep you feeling afraid and intimidated. Now we say this, and yet we know full well that there are individuals in your governments and in your law enforcement systems that mean well and that got into those professions with the best of intentions. And so, we are not speaking about individuals here. We are speaking about the system.

Your medical system, your health care system, is designed to make you dependent upon it for your health and well-being. Your economic system is designed to keep you in debt, to keep you from having enough. Your educational system is designed to keep you from independent thought. So knowing this, knowing that these systems were created to keep you divided, small, afraid, dependent, and unheard, what are you going to do? Attempts at rising up against the system will not work. Attempts to bring the systems down will not work.

Stepping outside of the system to create the world that you want to live in is what will work. And you do that on an individual level and on the level of community. This is why you do not need broad, sweeping changes to create the reality you prefer. You just need to be the light that burns outside of the system and attracts others to it with your beauty, with your honor, and with your love.

We are Michael. We are infinite. We are Love."

MOMENTARY GOALS

∞

"Welcome. We are here to serve and assist you.

In reevaluating your goals for this lifetime on a fairly regular basis, you open yourselves up to new possibilities. By setting aside goals that you created from a place of lack, you allow yourselves to experience more of who you are. As long as your goals are designed to compensate for something that you feel is missing in your lives, they will continue to perpetuate that experience of self.

So we recommend that you create goals for the moment you are in. In other words, you could say, 'My goal for this moment is to feel compassion for that person over there who is suffering.' And then you do it, and then in the next moment you create a goal for yourself to feel joy, freedom, or love.

And as you fulfill these goals moment to moment, you will find that the future that you were striving for is not so significant. You will find that you do not need to go anywhere, do anything, or create any sort of financial security to live how you want to live.

Goals are excellent when used appropriately. And so, make your goal to live in the moment and to experience the moment as you want to experience it. Let the future you off the hook, and give the current now moment you the experience that he or she really wants, with no agenda and no need to be or do anything else, not in your now and not in your future moment.

We are Michael. We are infinite. We are Love."

OBSERVING WITHOUT JUDGMENT

∞

"Welcome. We are here to serve and assist you.

The willingness to observe without judgment is a skill that you will all master as you shift into a fifth dimensional frequency state. Making an observation without getting triggered by it enables you to make an informed decision. Decisions that are made from that place of having just been triggered will not lead you to the place that you ultimately want to go.

We suggest that you make a habit of being in observation mode. We are not suggesting that you detach from your emotional bodies. But what we are saying is that you can set forth the intention to observe without judgment and simply be with whatever situation is before you, whether it is something you are witnessing in your own lives, in the lives of those close to you, or some news story you are aware of.

The ability to look upon a situation without needing for it to be right or wrong is a strength. It is empowering, and it puts you in a place where you are more likely to be of service to all beings involved. As soon as you judge and take a side, you are no longer being of service. But when you seek to be the light and the love that the situation is calling for, and you bring it without hesitation, you enable all parties involved to find that place of non-judgment and to reconcile the differences between them.

You are much more powerful in non-judgmental observation than you are in taking a side, gathering numbers, and seeking to defeat, no matter what it is. So give yourselves the opportunity to observe, to be of service, and to allow others to follow your example.

We are Michael. We are infinite. We are Love."

LETTING NEW PERSPECTIVES TAKE HOLD

∞

"Welcome. We are here to serve and assist you.

Before you open any gateway into your consciousness, you must allow for yourself to experience all that is before you in a new way. This requires you to stretch, to take yourselves beyond where you have believed you were capable of going. When you hear about upgrades, DNA activations, and the downloading of codes and information, you get very excited. You all enjoy these types of experiences. But what you can do on your own is so much more powerful than any thing or upgrade you could receive from those like us or from your extra-terrestrial friends.

The power that you have within you is the power to perceive from a new perspective that which already is. You exercise this power by granting yourselves permission to do so. If you are attached to seeing the world through one particular lens, you will limit your growth potential. And as soon as you allow for the new perspective to take hold, and as soon as you are willing to accept it, you open that gateway.

You become more of who you are. You create new pathways in your brains, and you know yourselves more as multidimensional beings. What we are suggesting that you do is let go of your firm grip on the version of reality that you have often clung to as being the one right way to see it, to know it, and to be in it.

When you are willing to take on a new perspective on something that is very old, something that has played out millions of times on planet earth, you not only open the gateway to your consciousness, but you allow others to do the same through the power of your example. And that is just the type of thing that creates a worldwide shift in consciousness.

We are Michael. We are infinite. We are Love."

HOW IT SERVES

∞

"Welcome. We are here to serve and assist you.

There will come a time when you will recognize every moment of your lives as having served you in a remarkable way. You will not question why something occurred because you will see immediately how it serves you, and you will move forward.

You will not need to analyze anything. You will not need to break it down, to try and understand it. It will be crystal clear to you why everything occurs in your experience, and you will know precisely what to do. This time is not so far off in the distant future for all of you. So, it is quite possible for you to begin to tap in to this type of experience in the here and now. It is much more of an intuitive knowing than it is a figuring-out process.

So the first step is always to let go of your mental processes around an occurrence in your life. Instead, sit with the feeling of it, and ask the feeling to evoke a knowing within you of how it serves you and how you can move forward from it.

Ask for your higher self to show you what your next step is. Ask for your higher self to show you how this event will catapult you into something else, something more desirable. When you allow yourselves to feel the energy behind a situation and your emotional response to it, you know more clearly what it is that you would like to be feeling, and the vibration of it is closer than you think.

The vibration is always available to you, and you are more likely to sense it when you allow yourselves sink deeply into the present moment, the present circumstance. And it is most easily accessed when you surrender, when you let go of your thought processes, and when you ask your higher self those important questions.

We are Michael. We are infinite. We are Love."

MINIMIZING THE EFFECTS OF TRAUMA

∞

"Welcome. We are here to serve and assist you.

Minimizing the effects of traumatic experiences in your lives is one of your biggest challenges. There is no telling how you are going to respond to certain scenarios. You cannot know this before you incarnate, because where you are before you incarnate is so very different vibrationally.

So you enter your physical Earth experience not knowing how you will experience trauma, but you do know that you will experience it. Some of you take on more than others. This is a choice made by the individual soul. So how do you minimize the effects of these traumatic experiences? It is very tricky business, because you walk a fine line between denial, or suppression, and full acceptance and integration. Minimizing the effects means that you move more quickly into the integrative experience.

And the way that you do this is by acknowledging what has occurred, being present with it, allowing yourselves to feel into it, and most importantly, by remembering to use your breath. Using your breath to move energy keeps you from staying stuck in the traumatic experience. It allows you to process through it with courage and strength. The breath reminds you of who you are. It empowers you, and it is something that is available to you in every moment of your existence as a physical being.

Recognize that you are powerful beings who choose to experience trauma so that you can feel who you really are, rising above whatever the circumstance is in your lives.

We are Michael. We are infinite. We are Love."

HOLDING DIFFERENT PERSPECTIVES

∞

"Welcome. We are here to serve and assist you.

By your own account, there are several different ways of approaching the same subject. You have all taken on different perspectives on the same subject in your one lifetime. So imagine how many perspectives you have held over all of your lifetimes. Imagine how many different ways you have perceived reality.

So why then would you ever want to cling to one perspective? Why would you ever limit yourself in that way? You all tend to get very serious when it comes to your beliefs, what you believe is true. But what if instead you looked at these various perspectives like you would varieties of ice cream? And so, if you are having a chocolate chip ice cream cone, and someone else is enjoying their butterscotch ice cream cone, you wouldn't see any point in trying to get the other person to go along with you in your enjoyment of chocolate chip. In that example, you can see the value of variety.

But if someone disagrees with you politically, some of you won't even want to be friends with that person anymore. If someone eats meat, and you are a strict vegetarian, you may not want to be friends with that person anymore. We understand that the examples we are giving may involve issues that are much nearer and dearer to your hearts than what flavor of ice cream you enjoy.

But we invite you to let go of the seriousness when it comes to these different perspectives, because we want you to enjoy your lives and we want you to allow others to enjoy theirs. And when you allow another to hold a perspective that is different from yours, you are giving Source Energy the opportunity to explore Itself in the widest variety of ways, and we think that is a very good perspective.

We are Michael. We are infinite. We are Love."

EMBRACE IT ALL

∞

"Welcome. We are here to serve and assist you.

Placing your attention on that which is bothering you is not an act of self-sabotage. By giving attention to something that is unpleasant from your perspective, you allow yourself to access the emotions that it was always meant to trigger. And giving yourself permission to experience that unpleasant thought and those uncomfortable emotions actually removes their power.

By refusing to look at something because it is unpleasant or unwanted, you are actually giving it more power over you, because in your refusal to look at something, you are expending energy. If you spent your entire life building walls to protect yourself from that which is unpleasant or unwanted, you would have no time left to live your life.

Instead, we recommend that you look directly at that which is bothering you, to let those emotions come to the surface so that they too can be experienced. And then it is possible for you to choose that which you want to give your attention to. That is when you demonstrate to yourself how powerful you are.

If you can allow everything to be as it comes to you, and if you can push none of it away, you will actually experience more choices of what you do want, because hidden behind the bothersome, unpleasant, and unwanted experiences are everything that your heart desires.

We are Michael. We are infinite. We are Love."

PEACE IN A HEARTBEAT

∞

"Welcome. We are here to serve and assist you.

Believing in a cause will ignite within you a spark of desire, and that desire is fueling your presence on planet Earth. When you are passionate about something, you are allowing a greater flow of your own energy. It is not important what you are passionate about, just so long as you are allowing that energy to flow.

When you have an event like the recent acts of violence on your world that have gotten so much attention, you begin to feel passionate for the cause of peace and harmony. If all of you could then allow the energy to flow that the spark of this desire has summoned forth, you would achieve peace on Earth instantaneously.

The only thing getting in the way of the flow of that energy is the way that you are processing all of it through your minds. You want to have the right perspective. You want to take the right approach. But the only way for you to allow the energy to flow towards that cause of peace and harmony is to let go of your thoughts and to open your hearts to the possibility that peace can be achieved in a heartbeat.

This requires surrender. You must surrender to what is and what has occurred. Everything else can and will be taken care of with no need for further thoughts or actions on the part of humanity.

We are Michael. We are infinite. We are Love."

CONCLUSIONS

∞

"Welcome. We are here to serve and assist you.

By the time that you are adults, you have arrived at many conclusions about life, and you have closed many doors as a result of your arrival at those conclusions. You cannot help but pick up some ideas along your way. Some of those ideas come to you from your parents. Some come to you from the media and your teachers. Others come from your own personal experiences.

Whatever conclusions you have come to are true from a certain perspective, but that does not mean that you must give in to them. That does not mean that you must create with them. When you are certain about something, make sure that you also are aware of how your certainty feels. Notice whether the conclusion you have reached is one that you feel good about.

Perhaps you don't feel good about a particular conclusion, but you want to. You want to feel good about that subject. Instead of attempting to arrive at a new or better conclusion, just go right for how it is you want to feel about that subject. Don't create there to be a certain number of steps that you must take in order to get to the new conclusion.

If you find the feeling place of what it is you want to experience regarding that particular subject, you will be able to access a myriad of new ideas about it. But be wary of any conclusion because they are so final, and what you are is expansive. What you are is infinite. Anything that you attach yourself to that is an endpoint is only going to hold you back as a creator being, and that is why those conclusions don't all feel the way you want to feel.

We are Michael. We are infinite. We are Love."

BEAUTY WITHIN TRAGEDY

∞

"Welcome. We are here to serve and assist you.

When you are taking stock of your lives, and you are able to discover the gifts within the tragedies, within the failures, within all of the ways in which your life has not measured up by your standards, you have actually exceeded all of the goals that you have ever set. You see, if you accomplished everything that you set out to do, and if you had everything that you have ever desired, you would not then be able to appreciate how much adversity, pain, and shortcomings have to give you.

They are not your badges of honor to be worn like war wounds. That is not what we are saying. We are simply asking you to look for the ways in which the detours, the obstacles, and the pitfalls have led you to something even better.

And when you take the moment of time that is required to appreciate all that you have around you, all that you may not have had without the tragedy or the failure, you are giving yourself so much more than any accomplishment could give you. You must be the one who decides what real success is in life. You must be the one to define success in your own terms. If you create the goal in order to get something so that you can then feel happy, you are missing the direct route.

The direct route to happiness is to find it within you. And you don't need to ignore anything in order to be happy. You don't need to pretend that things are different than how they actually are. When you look for the opportunity for beauty within tragedy, you have everything that you need, everything that could ever come from having a human experience on planet Earth.

We are Michael. We are infinite. We are Love."

BEING OF SERVICE TO ALL

∞

"Welcome. We are here to serve and assist you.

Your desire to serve others comes from that deep sense of knowing that you are not only connected to all others, but that you are one and the same. We are all the same being expressing in different form, in different frequency ranges. And when you reach that level of awareness, your inclination to serve becomes stronger. It becomes a heartfelt calling.

You are being given opportunities to know your oneness all of the time, and you either respond by accepting it or by denying it. The denial comes in part from religious programming. When you are taught that there is good and bad and that they will be separated for all of eternity, that keeps you from the knowing of oneness.

True service is to all humans, all beings. You would never deny an act of service to someone based on their beliefs, once you recognize that they are you and you are them. So in order for you to ultimately be of service to humanity, you must first let go of the idea of separation and of good and bad.

When you no longer see there to be a victim and a perpetrator, you can be of service to both. You can be of service to the one who is playing the victim and the one who is playing the perpetrator, and you can see the Divinity in each. You can sense the perfection in all of it, because you will have stepped out of judgment. You will have let go of polarity, and you will know yourselves yet again as the Source of all things.

We are Michael. We are infinite. We are Love."

THE NOW MOMENT

∞

"Welcome. We are here to serve and assist you.

Because there is only the now moment, you cannot possibly interpret the past or the future as it really was or really will be. You will always be perceiving that which is past or future to you from your now moment. The now moment is a filter of sorts, giving you only information that is pertinent to it. And so everything is a projection through that lens, or that filter, of where you are in that moment.

Your now moment could be described, in fact, as a vibration, because that is what everything is. It is a unique vibration. You create through vibration, and you perceive through vibration. Therefore, recognize that anything from your past that you believe is affecting you in your now is only doing so because of the now you are in. So it is quite accurate to say that they are affecting each other, but you do not need to go back and change your past in order to create a new now.

And the future that you will encounter will always be the result of the now moment as you experience it. One of the easiest ways for you to change your perception, and therefore your vibration, is through your focus. Focus on something in your now moment that is of a high frequency.

When you ask for our help in the archangel realm, or when you ask for the help of your guides or any other high-frequency being, the reason you receive it is because you have shifted your focus. The help is always there. The future you want to experience is always there, and it is only through the now moment that you can shift. So do not wait for a better future to shift it for you.

We are Michael. We are infinite. We are Love."

THE POWER OF LOVE

∞

"Welcome. We are here to serve and assist you.

Before you begin changing anything, take a look at it and offer your love and your appreciation for it. There is more to be gained from loving what is than there ever will be in changing what is into something else.

What you are living and who you are as individuals will always be changing into something more, but you often seek to accelerate the process. You look at what is, know that there is something more, and seek to use your powers as creator beings to change what is more rapidly.

There is nothing wrong with this, with exerting your abilities, your powers. But the power of unconditional love is stronger than the power to create a reality that elicits more love from you. So demonstrate to yourselves how powerful you are, not in your ability to create something else, something better, but in your ability to create yourselves as those who offer unconditional love.

Always begin with yourselves. Always seek to find the love within every situation and within every aspect of who you are. You cannot lose and you cannot fail when you make that your number one priority, when you seek love above change, above better, and above more.

We are Michael. We are infinite. We are Love."

PERCEPTION IS CREATIVE

∞

"Welcome. We are here to serve and assist you.

In your perception of reality, you are creating it. There are so many different ways to perceive the same thing, the same person, or the same event. It is you and only you who determines how you perceive the reality that is before you, and that decision is usually made without your conscious participation.

In other words, you are not usually deciding how to perceive your reality. More often than not, you let programming determine that perception. We want to be clear about one thing – you have chosen whatever programming you have received. So you are not a victim of that programming.

But once you wake up to it, you can then see it for what it is. And then you have the option of deciding how you want to perceive your reality. And that will determine what reality shows up in front of you.

So first of all, notice your perceptions. Notice how you have been choosing unconsciously to perceive your reality, and do so without judgment. And then decide that you can choose more consciously. You can see your reality differently in order to shift your experience of it.

This is one of the ways you shift into a reality that is more to your liking. The more that you decide to perceive your reality in a way that serves you, the better you become at creating a reality consciously that you will enjoy effortlessly.

We are Michael. We are infinite. We are Love."

NO WRONG WAY

∞

"Welcome. We are here to serve and assist you.

Ultimately, there is nothing that you can do wrong. There is no such thing as sin. There is not even the tiniest mistake that can be made. We are speaking now of the ideas that you have on your world of right and wrong. These are not absolutes. They are not determined by anything outside of you.

There is no right way to do something. There is no wrong answer. There is only that which serves you and that which does not. When we talk about serving you and not serving you, we are speaking now about the intentions that you hold. If you hold the intention of putting out a fire, then throwing gasoline on it does not serve you. Throwing water on it does.

So let us say that you come across a fire, and you want to put it out. And you do not know the difference between water and gasoline and their effects on fire. Let us say you throw the gasoline onto the fire, and let us say that you survive the experience. Now your intention to put out the fire is even stronger, and now the water is even more appreciated and the experience is more satisfying.

But you could have also thrown dirt on the fire or smothered it in some other way. And that is not a more right way to go about it. In fact, if you do not give yourself the experience of throwing the gasoline on the fire, then you are not having as much of a diverse experience as you could.

So if that is the underlying intention that you have before incarnating, then certainly it would not serve you to throw the water or the dirt onto the fire first. Diversity of experience is a wonderful thing. It is highly recommended. It is sought after and appreciated, and it always serves you.

We are Michael. We are infinite. We are Love."

THE NEGATIVE

∞

"Welcome. We are here to serve and assist you.

From your perspective, there are things, there are actions, and there are people who you would define as negative. You often label something as negative without really understanding what that means. What is negative? What does it mean to you? And most importantly, what do you do about it?

We suggest that instead of calling something or someone negative, you take note of how you feel. Put your attention there. That is how you are served by that which you are calling negative. You are given the opportunity to experience something within yourselves that you could not otherwise experience. And if you cannot experience an emotion like fear, sadness, anger, or despair, then you also cannot experience love, joy, freedom, or excitement.

Seeing as that is the case, can you not see how something negative could actually be considered positive? Can you not see the benefit of what you consider to be inherently negative? And if you are able to do this, if you are able to turn something negative around, you are then capable of getting to the emotion that you want to feel more quickly.

Now here comes the tricky part. You must allow that which you have deemed negative to be what it is, and you must allow it to trigger you in the way that it does. There is no need to pretend that something is not what it is, or that you don't feel how you do about it. That is a trap. So allow what is negative to be, allow yourselves to feel what you feel, and then derive the benefit of the experience by shifting your perspective.

We are Michael. We are infinite. We are Love."

THE DIVINITY IN ALL CHOICES

∞

"Welcome. We are here to serve and assist you.

In your progression through your lifetimes, you are giving yourselves similar choices so that you can see what each choice you make results in. So you may choose option A in one lifetime, option B in another lifetime, and so on.

When you think in terms of right and wrong choices and mistakes, you are thinking about your lives from a place of judgment. If instead you were to see and really know that every choice was necessary, you could take some of the pressure off of yourselves for making the right decision this time around.

You talk about learning from your mistakes. And when you do so, you seem to imply that the purpose of making the mistake was so that you would know not to make it again. But if instead the mistake was giving you an experience that you could not otherwise have, could you not see it as the right action to take? All of these various choices from your succession of incarnations allows you to have a fuller experience of who you are. So if you actually saw that as the purpose of your life, you would know that everything that you do or do not do serves you very well.

And when you draw from all of these experiences and all of the emotions that you have felt, you bring yourselves to a place where you recognize the Divinity in all choices and in all beings who are making those choices. And that recognition will allow you to release judgment, to live and let live, and to make your own choices fearlessly and without hesitation. That is truly how you live in the present moment with all of your power behind you.

We are Michael. We are infinite. We are Love."

UNCOVERING SECRETS

∞

"Welcome. We are here to serve and assist you.

When you are seeking to uncover what has always remained hidden from you, there is a vibration of struggle that you carry. Struggle only gets you more struggle. Therefore, allow those mysteries to remain as they are. Be not in such a hurry to find the secrets that you wish to know about.

All will come to you in perfect timing. There is no need for you to be anywhere that you are not, to know anything that you do not, or to come in contact with any beings that are not visible to you. But we know many of you desire to have more contact, to know more, and to see that which is hidden.

So we ask that you put aside those desires for the moment and reach for the feeling instead, not because the feeling will then manifest the information or the beings, but because the feeling is part of who you are. You have All That Is contained within you, and yet most of you are accessing a very small amount of that which is available. And what you seek outside of you is vast by comparison.

It is as though anything that you experience in your inner world is inherently less satisfying to you. And we want to encourage you to flip that belief around. Let your inner world be the most fascinating, the most real, and the most vivid of all your experiences.

We are Michael. We are infinite. We are Love."

FRESH PERSPECTIVES

∞

"Welcome. We are here to serve and assist you.

Something always brings you a deeper understanding of that which was once before just a concept to you. Something will happen in your lives to give you a more personal perspective, and a more personal experience of that which seemed foreign and like it had nothing to do with you. This is the process of becoming.

It is in the living of your lives that you do all of your spiritual work. You have spiritual practices and you have experiences that you take from those practices. And these are the things you tell your friends about. These are the things you believe are furthering your evolution. But nothing furthers your evolution like experience, especially experience that causes you to come face-to-face with a judgment.

When you can see yourselves as no different and no better than anyone else, you gather up a piece of yourselves and bring it home. When you have one of these experiences we are talking about, you get to see it from a fresh perspective. You get to see how it is possible for anyone to do something, or to believe something, or to say something.

And when you have that perspective, you can release your judgment, you can let go of blame and criticism. You can see everything for what it is. It is all a choice for an experience. And you are all making the choice. When you let go of the idea of good and bad and right and wrong. When you allow everyone to choose their experience, then you will know that you have become more of who you are.

You will become unconditional in your love and unconditional in your acceptance. You will find it much easier to maintain your frequency no matter what is happening around you, because you will see no need and no value in condemnation. You will see no need to make any experience less than any other. And when come to that point, you can create any experience you desire.

We are Michael. We are infinite. We are Love."

EXPERIENCING ALL ANGLES

∞

"Welcome. We are here to serve and assist you.

In order for you to experience something fully, you must experience it from all angles. This is what you all decided to do before incarnating on planet Earth. You decided to experience all that you could in a human body, from every imaginable perspective.

And this is what you have done over the course of your many lifetimes on planet Earth. So everything that you see happening in the world today - every injustice, every act of violence, and every joyous occasion - have all been experienced by you in some incarnation. And so whatever it is that you find abhorrent, and whatever it is that you would love to experience but do not believe that you can, you have already experienced these things. If you hadn't, you would be experiencing them in this current lifetime.

What we suggest that all of you do is look around and decide that you are going to accept all that is and is not in your life and all that is happening in the world today. As you do, you welcome a part of yourself home, you become more whole, and you release trauma.

You are living in this lifetime in service to all of your other lifetimes. And as you recognize that, you can see and understand how everything that is and is not is of service to you. So be willing to engage with your world with this knowing. And in so doing, you release all resistance, and you welcome all aspects of yourself home. This is truly how you live as a divine Being in a physical body.

We are Michael. We are infinite. We are Love."

THE NEW PERSPECTIVE

∞

"Welcome. We are here to serve and assist you.

In the shifting of your consciousness, you have taken on a different perspective. The new perspective allows for there to be greater diversity. The new perspective allows others to make choices that are different from yours. The new perspective is not one of control. It is not one of need.

In your creation of the new perspective that you have taken on, you have not needed to abolish any of the old perspectives. You have not needed to bury them underneath anything to make them go away. This is worth recognizing and noting because in your creation of the new, there is no need for you to destroy that which has been.

There is no need for you to take down any person, any religion, any corporation, or any government. They all still get to exist in the new reality, but you do not have to choose to experience any of them. So the new perspective that you are taking on is inclusive. It does not see itself as better, and it does not see any other perspective as worse.

The new perspective that you are taking on recognizes that it is in a constant state of change and it accepts that. There is no need to cling. There is no need to write down lists of rules and regulations. There is more flexibility in your new perspective. There is more room for growth, more room for experience, and ultimately, more room for love.

Love gives you the ability to hold more than one perspective at once, to see them both as valid, and to see yourself as simply the experiencer. That which you are shifting to creates new opportunities for knowing yourselves as all perspectives, and that is the ultimate in expansion.

We are Michael. We are infinite. We are Love."

IT ALL SERVES YOU

∞

"Welcome. We are here to serve and assist you.

Putting yourself in various situations always leaves you with a feeling that you are not actually in control. The results of your participation in circumstances that are not of your choosing are always positive.

By now, you will have had several experiences in your lives that you never would have asked to experience. And by now you have recognized the value that you received from most of those experiences. There are undoubtedly still a few holdouts.

It is important for you to acknowledge how everything that you have experienced has served you. Not only will you receive the full benefit of having had those experiences, but in so doing you remind yourselves that not everything that comes your way is going to have whipped cream and a cherry on top. Those are the experiences that grab your attention. Those are the experiences that help you awaken.

Not everything along your path that serves you must also be unpleasant and unwanted. We just want to point out that those unpleasant, unwanted life circumstances are filled with the energy that will propel you into the fifth dimension.

So look not to create a perfect life by your standards and definitions. Look instead to find the perfection in the life you are living. See it all as a wondrous journey that includes peaks and valleys. And you will always shine brightest, even after getting dragged through the muck and the mire.

We are Michael. We are infinite. We are Love."

TRUE ESSENCE

∞

"Welcome. We are here to serve and assist you.

Everyone that you encounter is a person that deserves your full attention. You would appreciate who it was you were interacting with more if you could see their true essence. If you knew that the homeless person on the street was an angel in disguise, you would have a bit more reverence for that individual.

When you interact with anyone, regardless of who they are to you, give your attention to their true essence. Now that essence may be shrouded, but it is still there. We are not asking you to overlook what it is that the person is saying or doing, as though those things do not matter. We are simply asking that you consider the Source.

Recognize that the distortions through which the light is shining are not the truth of who that being really is. Be willing to address what they are offering to you, while simultaneously holding your focus on the essence of who they are.

This awareness will also serve you when you turn your attention back to self. You are also a high-frequency being of light and love expressing in human form, and you deserve to give yourself that same respect and reverence as you would if you could see the true essence of who you are.

We also encourage you to view everything around you as a miracle. All That Is expressing Itself in form is a miraculous event. Be willing to look deeper. What you see on the surface is a projection. All that you see is Love in some form, in some format. And it is all there in service to the Light that you are. Remember and remind yourselves of this on a more frequent basis as you move through this journey.

We are Michael. We are infinite. We are Love."

RELEASING RESISTANCE
IN THE INFORMATION AGE

∞

"Welcome. We are here to serve and assist you.

Because you are lessening your resistance to that which is and has been in your world, you are experiencing your shift with more ease. Because it is easier to simply release or reduce your resistance to something than to eradicate it, you are becoming more whole every day.

You cannot eradicate something within yourself, even if you were to somehow find a way to eliminate it outside of yourself. You would only be doing so temporarily, because nothing can be completely eliminated. It can be deactivated, however. And that is what you do when you release resistance and accept the presence of something that you do not like and that you do not want.

The way in which you are releasing resistance is through your information age. Not only is everything right in your face on your computers, and your televisions, and your phones, but you also get to see a variety of perspectives on this thing that you cannot ignore. The offering of those perspectives by others opens the doorway for you to have a new perspective of your own, one which carries with it less resistance, less fear, and less judgment.

So when you see things happening in your world that make it look as though you are regressing as a species, just realize that the events are giving you the opportunity to let go of some of that resistance, some of that fear, and some of that judgment. And by looking directly at it, you cannot help but do so. You cannot hold those lower frequencies anymore, not if you want to remain in this physical reality.

We are Michael. We are infinite. We are Love."

The Seventh Sign

∞

You Now Know
Who You Really Are

YOU ARE EVERYTHING

∞

"Welcome. We are here to serve and assist you.

It will always serve you to look within yourselves, and it doesn't matter what you find. It serves you to look, and it serves you to find. It serves you to feel, and it serves you to desire.

There is no right and wrong, and this is especially true when it comes to your inner world. In fact all of the problems that you face stem from your shame and your suppression of that which you find within yourselves.

So exploring your inner world with no desire to change or fix anything that you find, is the ultimate in evolution. Your evolution does not preclude you from feeling things or from being a certain way. Your evolution is all about letting go of the shame and the judgment.

Because no matter who you are in this lifetime, no matter how saintly, you have played the role of the villain, somewhere and somewhen. And until you make peace with that part of you that still exists and always will, there's no amount of cleansing that can free you from your own judgment. And no matter how adept you become at creating your reality, you cannot create yourselves to be other than everything.

You are all inclusive. So you might as well seek out all parts of yourselves with curiosity and with a desire to be loving and compassionate to all that you are, no matter what you find and no matter what you feel. You are Source Energy Beings, and Source Energy is all that is.

We are Michael. We are infinite. We are Love."

YOU AS THE UNIVERSE

∞

"Welcome. We are here to serve and assist you.

Believing in your ability to stretch yourselves beyond where you have been before is what you are about to accomplish. We are not talking about believing in your abilities to manifest, or to connect with your guides, or to have any type of supernatural power. The ability that we are referring to is the ability to perceive yourselves as the universe you once thought you inhabited.

This is the leap of faith that is necessary for you to manifest, for you to have all of the other powers and abilities that you seek. Even your willingness to see your guides as aspects of you will give you that connection that you desire.

As long as you see the universe as something outside of you that you exist within, you make it harder on yourselves. You put yourselves up against forces that also must exist outside of you. But as you begin to see yourselves as the only force, and as you begin to see the universe as a part of that force that you are, you will have the ease that you seek and you will enjoy your existence beyond measure.

So how do you accomplish this? How do you awaken to this knowing? Start by interacting with your world differently. See everything as an inside job. Talk to the universe in the same way that you talk to yourself, with full recognition that you are being heard. Seek to expand your consciousness, and do so by feeling for what is around you before interacting with it in any other way. Begin to experience all of it as you, expressing in another physical form.

We are Michael. We are infinite. We are Love."

YOU ARE THE PURPOSE

∞

"Welcome. We are here to serve and assist you.

You are the most advanced version of yourself that you have ever been. You are taking consciousness somewhere that consciousness has never been. The only requirement of you in the completing of this task is that you remain focused here and now.

You are not proving yourself to anyone, nor is it necessary for you to accomplish anything in order to take consciousness where it has never been before. Your awareness that you are in fact doing this is not even required. Most of what you experience in your day-to-day lives has deeper significance and meaning than you will ever be able to comprehend.

And that is quite all right, because living your life is also important. By being present with your life and with the circumstances of your life, you are moving yourself further and further along. You need not step outside of your life and what it is bringing to you in order for you to really get it and expand in the way that you are already naturally doing.

Purpose is a big question and concern for so many of you because you feel that in order for your life to have value, you must be doing something to save the world or to help others. This is part of a program that you are all buying into. That program says that only those of you who are making a difference on a large scale are really living your purpose for being here.

You are the purpose. Your unique circumstances are necessary to give consciousness what it is seeking. Having no idea what you're doing is perfectly acceptable. Take for granted that you are exactly where you are supposed to be, doing exactly what you are supposed to be doing and let the only variable be how much you are infusing your light into what you are already living.

We are Michael. We are infinite. We are Love."

TRUTH

∞

"Welcome. We are here to serve and assist you.

Telling yourself the truth will always set you free. Being in alignment with your truth will always serve you. Knowing that there is no one truth that will resonate with all of you will allow you to allow others to believe what they believe. And that will also set you free.

Having the right perspective is a burden. Recognizing that your perspective is unique to you puts you in a state of grace. Leaving the debates to those who wish to debate is yet another act of allowing. Taking yourself from a debate in order to allow another to live by their own truth will set you free from further debates.

Knowing that the only truth is that you are all expressions of All That Is puts everything into its proper perspective. How you live is your truth. Deciding that your truth can change from one moment to the next gives you the opportunity to explore more of who you are and more of All That Is.

Being true to yourself is an expression of self-love. Clinging to a truth only limits you and stagnates your growth. You are truth. You express who you are, and that is truly a gift. Everything else is just words, and beliefs, and thoughts. And they are true to themselves, but not necessarily to you.

We are Michael. We are infinite. We are love."

EXPLORING LABELS

∞

"Welcome. We are here to serve and assist you.

Labeling creates more of the illusion of separation. When you put someone or something in a box and then place a label on that box, you are only permitting them to be that which is on the label. And you are denying yourself the opportunity to see that being, that object, that ideology as being contained within you and as serving you in some way.

The labels that you have come up with do not begin to encapsulate what that being, that object, or that ideology really is. Your label is your perspective, and your perspective can and does change. But changing your perspective does not mean that you then must take whatever you have placed in the box out so that you can put a kinder, happier label upon it.

Change your perspective by turning whatever it is you are looking at around and seeing yourself. Your perspective on yourself is reflected in the label that you apply to most things. Therefore, we suggest that you first acknowledge that you are all things and that all things are contained within you. Whether they are active in this moment or not, they are there.

We know that you desire to be that which you would deem 'good.' And you certainly have the right to express whatever part of yourself that you want to express. We ask that you allow others to do the same. So instead of thinking to yourself, 'So and so is a certain way,' say to yourselves, 'So and so is exploring that.' And allow yourself the freedom to explore as well.

Allow yourself to access that which you have been afraid to explore. You will still be able to choose that which you want to be, but at least you will have the experience of having explored all that you are.

We are Michael. We are infinite. We are Love."

YOU ARE AN EXPRESSION OF SOURCE

∞

"Welcome. We are here to serve and assist you.

Zeroing in on what you want often gives you the sense of satisfaction that you are seeking from your lives. Being able to receive that which you have determined is valuable gives you more of that sense of satisfaction. Taking your lessons in life as though they were badges of honor is another way to engage with a sense of satisfaction.

No matter what it is that you are seeking, you will find that satisfaction is at the core of each desire. You all seek a sense of completion. You all want to know that you have gotten all that there was to get out of life, no matter what it is that you are seeking.

All satisfaction that you are looking for comes from a perspective that you hold. You can easily obtain the satisfaction that you seek without ever having to achieve, or obtain, or experience a single thing. Deep satisfaction comes from knowing that you are a Source Energy expression.

That kind of knowing will never be obtained by looking outside of yourselves for the evidence, whether you are looking for the evidence from relationships, material wealth, or spiritual enlightenment. You'll always be able to tell yourselves that there is more. You will always fall short.

Knowing yourselves as Source Energy is not complicated. It does not involve years and years of spiritual practice. It is a simple acknowledgement, and you are the only one who can give it to yourselves. Take a moment to tell yourself that you are an expression of Source Energy.

Feel where that hits you in your body. See if you can take it again, and again, and again until you are satisfied, until you are filled with that knowing. And then enjoy your life, rather than seeking something in your life to confirm to you the most important truth in the universe.

We are Michael. We are infinite. We are Love."

LETTING GO OF ILLUSION

∞

"Welcome. We are here to serve and assist you.

Letting go of the illusion does not mean that you stop living your lives. It does not mean that you transcend this reality. Letting go of the illusion is letting go of the idea that you are somehow limited to this experience and to your body.

When you let go of those illusions, you then begin to operate as a being who is exploring your life using a body to do so. You recognize that you are not your body, but you do not dismiss your body. You embrace the body that you are working with and see it as the perfect vehicle for you to do what you set out to do by incarnating.

You also recognize that your life is not the time that you spend contained within a body. You recognize that the experiences that you have while working with your particular body are part of a much bigger story and that they do not define you. You define them. Your life experiences do not give your life meaning. You give meaning to your life experiences.

By letting go of the illusion, you set yourselves free from limitation, and you know yourselves more fully and more accurately as beings of light and love who are focusing on a very particular set of circumstances. And you use those circumstances to better know yourselves, experientially. Give yourselves a chance to let go and still remain focused on the illusion that you have created specifically for you.

We are Michael. We are infinite. We are Love."

THE SOURCE ENERGY PERSPECTIVE
∞

"Welcome. We are here to serve and assist you.

By living your life, you are letting Source Energy play through you. You are giving Source Energy an opportunity for new experience. Therefore, live your life and recognize that this is precisely what is happening. Believing this is one thing. It is nice to come to this awareness and to hold that knowing in your mental body.

But to live it, to truly embody it, that is what you are all here to do. That is what you are all sorting out. You may find that the challenge lies not within knowing that you are allowing Source Energy to have an experience through you, but in synching up with that perspective of Source as you go through the motions of your day.

Every act is an opportunity to know yourself as Source and to see something through the eyes of Source for the very first time. Taking on the perspective of Source is as easy as deciding that it is the perspective that you would like to hold. Because remember, you already are Source. And sometimes, many times in fact, you are simply pretending to be something else, something separate, or less, than who and what you really are.

And every time that you acknowledge your true identity as a Source Energy Being, filtering Its way through a physical experience, you make it easier for yourself and others to hold that perspective. And the more of you who hold that perspective, the more you create Heaven on Earth. Be willing to don the perspective of who you really are and to live your life in that vibration.

We are Michael. We are infinite. We are Love."

A COSMIC JOKE

∞

"Welcome. We are here to serve and assist you.

By taking yourselves too seriously, you limit the amount of joy that is available to you. By letting yourselves see all of this as a fun adventure, you will notice that there is so much less to be serious about. As you observe your life, the lives of those around you, and the world at large, look for the humor in what is happening.

See the absurdity as a cause for laughter. Make fun of what is happening. Your spirituality does not have to be a place where only serious thoughts and discussions are allowed. You have been taught to believe that things of a Divine nature are to be revered, but that was always just a tactic to keep you in your place.

As you recognize yourself as a Divine Creation, and you see how playfully and carefully you have selected the details of your life, you can see the humor in it. Certainly a god who cannot pay the rent is a cosmic joke. As you take on that perspective of lightness and humor, you see the various situations in your life, in your world, and in the lives of those around you as not so serious at all.

You see it all for what it is – it is a game that you are playing. And as real as it seems, it is still meant to be fun. And the ones who are having the most fun are the ones who are deciding that all of this can be fun, even with the tragedies, and the loss, and the heartbreak. You are all beings of light, so having a lighthearted approach to your life is allowing yourselves to be as you truly are.

We are Michael. We are infinite. We are Love."

ALL ABOUT LOVE

∞

"Welcome. We are here to serve and assist you.

Love welcomes you into its arms, giving always. Love is always available. You come from love. You are Love, and love is where you are going. Take a moment now to breathe. Breathe in some of that love that is calling you home and welcome it as it welcomes you.

Sending love to yourself is somewhat of a fantasy. But you get the idea when we tell you to do this. A funny thing about it is that love is all around you. It is inside of you. It is constantly being sent to you, and it is beckoning you home. So when we say, 'Send yourself some love,' what we really mean is, 'Acknowledge yourself as love.'

Tune yourself to the Love that you are and feel it in your bones. More often than not, you are holding back love, not only from yourselves, but from others. This is a part of the idea of separation that you are all playing out. For to be separate means that you could and do experience yourselves as something other than love.

But love is the basis of all things. It is the basis of all actions, all desires. It is not as though you need to find love, and you certainly do not need to find anyone to love you. But holding yourselves in a frequency of love is truly an act of returning to your origin.

And from your state of ever-flowing, unconditional love, you are able to create anything and everything, because anything that you can imagine and everything that is was created with love, out of love, and for the sake of love. You are an experiment in love, and now is the time for you to prove the hypothesis.

We are Michael. We are infinite. We are Love."

LETTING GO OF DEFINITIONS

∞

"Welcome. We are here to serve and assist you.

Take away all that you have used to define yourselves. Take it away voluntarily and with the intention of knowing the deeper, more natural, and truer idea of who you are. Let go of your definitions, your accomplishments, your strengths. Let go of your nationalities, your beliefs, even your gender. Let go of it all, and as you do, you will find that a weight is lifted. When you are not concerned with how you are defining yourself or with how someone else is looking at you, you will experience a freedom unlike any you have experienced before. You will know yourselves as infinite, limitless, and brimming with potential for even more.

We ask you to take part in this un-defining, this deconstruction, because we want you to have an easier time with what is well underway. We want you to enjoy now all that life has to offer. And we realize that you cannot do that as you cling to the old ways, the old models, the old systems and paradigms. Included in all of that is the idea that a person could know who you are by looking at a sheet of paper with all of your vital statistics and other fun facts about you. We are not just talking about going beyond the physical here. We are talking about going beyond all labels, all of your history, even that which you think you prefer.

As you strip yourselves down to your core, to the essence of who you are, you emerge from the soil like a sapling, firmly rooted in this reality, but with so much more potential than this reality and the way that it is structured could ever provide. As you navigate through your labels and definitions, be sure to release them lovingly, for they have served you.

And give yourselves the freedom to not only seek out more of who you have ever dreamt that you could be, but also the freedom to exist from one moment to the next with no attachment – no attachment to what you just said or did or believed yourselves to be. This is the fifth dimensional way of knowing and expressing who you are.

We are Michael. We are infinite. We are Love."

YOU AND YOUR UNIVERSE

∞

"Welcome. We are here to serve and assist you.

By living what you are now you are sending the preferences to all dimensions. You are having an impact on more than just your time/space reality. You are constantly sending out signals to all beings in this universe and beyond. Therefore give yourselves plenty of credit for everything that you live. Acknowledge yourselves often for having contributed mightily to this universe, not in your accomplishments, not in your creations, not even so much in your acts of service. You contribute with your willingness to be here and to traverse your reality of polarity with courage and grace.

We see you living your lives, feeling insignificant, and seeking something more for yourselves, seeking to do more, to contribute more, to have a bigger impact. And in those moments, we want so much to show you the impact that you are having. But it is not possible to demonstrate to you. You would not be able to see it with your eyes.

The universe is taking shape around you. It is finding new ways to be. It is welcoming all of your input, and it hears all of your requests. Be willing to have a more interactive relationship with your universe. Be willing to communicate, to ask, and to send out your unique preferences. But do so in an act of collaboration and co-creation. Demands are never met. But when you see yourself as an equal to this universe, then you have some ground to stand on. Then you can begin to notice how the universe responds to you in the same way that you respond to it. It holds you with as much reverence. It seeks to understand you. It marvels at how expansive you are.

And yes, you and your universe are one. But you are playing, and you are playing with the idea that you exist in it. So have fun with that game, and know that the rules are always changing to accommodate you in your quest of self-discovery.

We are Michael. We are infinite. We are Love."

EMPTINESS

∞

"Welcome. We are here to serve and assist you.

Everyone feels emptiness from time to time. It is part of your wholeness. When you feel empty inside, you usually think that you have been abandoned. That is how emptiness feels. You feel separate. You feel alone. You feel dark and despair. Emptiness, as an experience, can be seen as a cleanse.

Just as you would cleanse your physical body, you can cleanse your energetic body, and emptiness is your way of doing it. Imagine pulling the plug on a drain and letting all the water flow down the pipes. The water is taking with it all the dirt and the oils and the hair that you no longer need. Emptiness, if you happen to be experiencing it, is not something to be avoided, is not something to fear.

It is a reminder that you are more than what you have built yourselves up to be. Therefore, be open to the experience of having everything stripped away, including the others who you feel closest to, so that you can have an energetic cleanse and so that you can bring forth more light to fill that empty space.

Take yourselves into the void, knowing that your experience of it does not create more void and emptiness. But instead, you allow more of that which you are to fill in the gaps left behind by that which you are not, by that which is temporary. This is how you build your fifth dimensional selves.

We are Michael. We are infinite. We are Love."

THE PRIMARY MANIFESTATION

∞

"Welcome. We are here to serve and assist you.

Always do your best to accentuate that which is serving you about your current situation in life. Looking for ways to let yourself off the hook will also serve you very well. We understand how knowing that you are creator beings can be both an exciting piece of news and burdensome at the same time.

We are giving you permission to let go of the need to know why something is manifesting in your life in the precise way that it is and why other things are not manifesting at all. Be willing to throw the need to know why out the window. And instead begin to see your life and all aspects of it as the perfect creation, giving you exactly what you need to move forward and to become the Being that you were always destined to be.

You are the primary manifestation of your life. You, and all of your wonderful gifts, far outweigh anything that you could manifest in your reality. And so, live your lives with that knowing – the knowing that your being here in the form that you are is the greatest accomplishment that you could ever achieve. Look with wonder upon yourselves and know that as perfect as you are, your life is bringing more of you forth to meet it.

And that is the most exciting piece of news you could ever receive, because you are the manifestation of everything that you have ever sought and that you could ever have. We welcome you to this beautiful creation that stands before you in the mirror and invites you to explore all the beauty, all the wonder, and all the majesty that you are in this very moment.

We are Michael. We are infinite. We are Love."

SEEKING, FINDING AND INTEGRATING

∞

"Welcome. We are her serve and assist you.

Seeking is so fundamental to your nature that you would find no joy in having everything, or knowing everything, because you would no longer have any reason to seek. Even Source seeks to know Itself, to expand, and to express the Love that It is. And you, as aspects of Source, are doing exactly that on a slightly smaller scale. But seek you will, seek you must, and only through seeking will you discover more of who you are.

There comes a time when you need to rest. There comes a time when you simply integrate that which you have discovered. So when you are in one of those phases, many of you become uncomfortable. You don't know why you are not feeling driven, and you seek to seek once again. So if you find yourself in one of these phases, or cycles of rest, do not worry that it might mean that you are coming to an end. The desire will once again bubble up within you when the timing is right.

And when it comes to finding what you are seeking, that is also coming in the perfect timing. So when you are in seeking mode, worry not that you will never find what you seek. Enjoy the journey. Enjoy the exploration. Enjoy that feeling when you know you are close, when you can feel the essence of what you seek in your bones. Those are the most delicious times for all of you.

And we delight in witnessing you seeking, finding, and integrating more of who you are. Everything that you seek is something that you already are. And knowing that can make the journey all the more enjoyable.

We are Michael. We are infinite. We are Love."

YOU ARE ALL HEROES

∞

"Welcome. We are here to serve and assist you.

That which is often difficult for you to hear is the greatest thing that you could ever absorb. That which is easy for you to hear often has very little impact on you. You are uncovering parts of yourselves that have remained hidden, or dormant, for eons and eons of your time. And as you encounter these aspects of who you are, you may find that they are hard to look at.

You may wonder why it has to be so challenging to do the work that you are doing. You may wonder why this evolution business, this ascension process, could not be a bit easier. And you may wonder if it is all worth it. Why not just push that emotion back down? Why not just ignore that which you do not want to see? We will tell you why. It is because you are accepting your roles as the heroes of your own stories.

What is a hero, but one who is willing to face the unthinkable, the unimaginable, the insurmountable? The hero is given the most challenging of challenges, and the hero stands tall in the face of these challenges. The hero is not really defeating anything or anyone. That is a misinterpretation of the stories you are given. They are not about squashing out the evil. They are about facing that which is a part of you and being willing to look it in the eye. Once you do that, you have already won.

You are all heroes, simply for being here at this time. And for recognizing your strengths, your willingness, and your courage, you embody the heroes that you have often seen portrayed in your movies and in your stories. There is not one of you who has not faced enormous challenge, and all of you are discovering what you are made of. That is a true victory. That is why you create the challenge.

We are Michael. We are infinite. We are Love."

LOSING YOURSELF

∞

"Welcome. We are here to serve and assist you.

Losing yourself in an activity welcomes a new you to emerge. All activities that you engage in offer you the opportunity to lose yourselves. And when you do, the you that emerges on the other side contains all that you were and more.

If there is something that you do that allows you to feel free and fully engaged at the same time, then this is something that you need to do often. Whether or not you think you have time to do the things that you lose yourselves in, you do have the time. But if you are not making time to do those things, then it is because you are clinging to the current version of yourself that you experience.

As much as you enjoy participating in activities where you lose yourselves, you also fear that 'losing yourself' means losing your identity. As many of you know, your identity is not comprised of your social security number, birthdate, name, country, and so on. Your identity is much larger than all the ways in which you could define it.

But having witnessed all of you and noticing the way you cling to various aspects of yourselves, we just want to say that it would behoove all of you to free yourselves from the concept of identity. The idea that anything could define you is a limitation. So lose yourselves, let go of your identities, and be willing to get lost, for that is the only way you will ever truly find yourselves.

We are Michael. We are infinite. We are Love."

YOUR LIFE'S PURPOSE

∞

"Welcome. We are here to serve and assist you.

Presenting your side of the story is also giving another the opportunity to expand into a new awareness. There is no purpose in holding back anything that you are feeling, that you are experiencing. It will not serve you in the long run to do so, because your perspective is worthy of Source Energy's attention. And if Source Energy believes that your side of the story is worth experiencing, then maybe you can believe that it is worthy of expression.

Some of you wonder what your purpose is in life. And immediately, you look to an action, a career, something tangible, or something you can do or contribute. Why not start by contributing your perspective a little more?

Your purpose is to exist as the unique expression of Source Energy that you are. What you do is not as important as what you are, but what you do tends to get all of the attention. Allow yourselves the luxury of feeling that your existence is your purpose. Your existence is unique, and your existence is worthy of expression.

You are not here to follow, and you are not really here to lead either. You are simply here to be yourselves, to let everyone else do the same, and to bring that which you are out in the open so that others may experience the majesty and the wonder of all that you are and be enriched by their exposure to you.

We are Michael. We are infinite. We are Love."

FEEL YOUR DIVINITY

∞

"Welcome. We are here to serve and assist you.

There will be no test administered. There is no standard that has been set. You are all making up the rules as you go. So there is no need for any of you to worry about whether you are hitting all the right marks. The idea that you are being judged, or measured against some standard, has in some ways been carried over to the spiritual and new age realm from religions.

We do not want to take any shots here at religion. It serves many people. But the one aspect of religion that keeps individuals separate and lower than God is this idea that there are rules set by God and standards that must be met. And we want all of you to leave that behind. We want all of you to acknowledge yourselves as that which you call God and to recognize that this is somewhat of a game you are playing with yourselves.

So when you look at yourself during meditation and decide that you are not doing a very good job, just relax and laugh. That is not what meditation is about. It is not about achieving perfection, nor is yoga, nor is any spiritual practice. They are about enjoying your connection and knowing of self as Divine. And if you are using them as such, then you get an A+ in our book.

Any thoughts of not living up to a standard can easily be released by you now that you are aware that you sometimes do this. And now that you know that, the only thing worth doing at this point is all that encourages you to feel your connection and the spark of Divinity within you. This is not a pass/fail examination. Enjoy the moments that have. Enjoy the feelings as they come, and experience all that you are, however brief those moments are, however rarely they come. Be pleased with every glimpse.

We are Michael. We are infinite. We are Love."

ACKNOWLEDGE YOURSELVES

∞

"Welcome. We are here to serve and assist you.

If we were to give you one piece of advice to live by and to apply to everything that you are living, we would tell you to give yourselves more credit. If you were to give yourselves more acknowledgement, more praise, more love, you would see instant results in your live. Not only would you enjoy your lives more, and not only would you feel better all that time, but that which is the reflection of your world would immediately show you how much it has to give.

Giving yourselves the credit that you deserve does not mean that you have to tally up all of your accomplishments and praise each one. It means that you acknowledge the light that is you. The light that is you does not need to accomplish or achieve anything. The light that is you simply is. You are all gifts unto this world. Your gifts are not your talents. Your gifts are your being-ness. Your mere existence is a gift.

So many of you want to do something with your lives. You want to find your calling and your purpose, and you want to take the necessary action steps to get to where you want to go. You want the world to acknowledge your light before you do. But what we recommend is that you look within yourselves for the light that you are, and without changing a thing, you give yourselves that acknowledgement and that credit and that love for simply existing as you are.

And then by all means be the light that you are, shine the light that you are, extend the light that you are out as far as you can. Stop looking for your purpose. Look for the light that you are. Become your biggest fan. Be willing to let yourselves off the hook. Be willing to measure your success by how much you are acknowledging yourselves in the here and now for the unique expression of Source that you are, and for no other reason than that.

And everything that you do and say and are will follow from that acknowledgement. And you will shine. And others will notice. And you will show them how to find and acknowledge their own.

We are Michael. We are infinite. We are Love."

EXPRESS YOURSELVES

∞

"Welcome. We are here to serve and assist you.

We provide you with our energy because we seek only to express that which we are. We are not seeking to fix any of you. We are not providing you with our insights because we see that you are lacking such insights. We are not doing any of this from a place of feeling that there is a lack of understanding on your part. We simply see you all as your true selves. And from that knowing of who you really are, we speak to you, we remind you, we call you into that knowing.

But it is inevitable that you will fully realize who and what you are and embody that energy on a daily and moment-to-moment basis. So we are not a necessary component in your evolution. But because we enjoy speaking our truth and because we enjoy connecting with all of you energetically, we provide you with our perspective.

Now, what if your life were lived in the same way? What if you decided that you did what you did not out of a need, not because you saw that something was lacking in your world? But what if you did what you did out of a desire to express that which you are? What then? How would your life be different? How would you be different?

When you talk about your purpose for being here, many of you consider what is needed and how you can fill the need. But we want to encourage you instead to look within yourselves and to let your light shine in whatever way you feel inspired to let it shine in each and every moment.

And when you string those moments together, if it does not look like you are doing something that you can put your finger on and say, 'This is what I do,' then that does not mean you are still looking for your purpose. That just means that your purpose presents itself to you in each and every moment, and you rise to the occasion by being who you are.

We are Michael. We are infinite. We are Love."

ACCESSING YOUR ENERGY

∞

"Welcome. We are here to serve and assist you.

Begin exercising your right to your own energy. Let everyone else off the hook, and give yourself what is rightfully yours. There is a tendency in all of you to look around at the world outside of you and to attempt to fill yourself with energy. You do this in any number of ways. Some of you have addictions that don't even look like addictions to most of the world. But all addictions are about energy and about the use or abuse of energy.

So finding your energy source is as simple as imagining that you have a valve inside of yourself and loosening the valve so that you can allow more energy to flow from within you, filling not only your physical structure, but also your energetic field. That energy that belongs to you IS you. It is not separate from you. It is not something that you need to access from another realm or another dimension. You are here and now, and so is the energy that you are.

But it is necessary for you to give yourselves that energy. It is a part of your evolution to recognize this and to let go of some of your outside energy sources. Some of you are doing this consciously. Others are having those sources taken away. But they are still calling the shots, just not from the level at which they operate. So you see, knowing yourselves as your higher selves will make it easier on you to access the energy that is you.

But as long as you know yourselves as separate, as egoic, you will still attempt to receive that which feeds and nurtures you from somewhere, something, or someone. Believe us when we say that there's more to you than meets the eye, that the source that is you is infinite, and that the valve is always there, ready and waiting to be loosened, to open the floodgates, and to allow yourselves expansion from within.

We are Michael. We are infinite. We are Love."

THE VOLUME CONTROL

∞

"Welcome. We are here to serve and assist you.

Which way you express the love that you are is your choice. That you express the love that you are is not a choice. Because you are Love incarnate, you have no choice and no say in whether or not you are who you are. But you certainly can turn the volume down or turn the volume up.

We envy you for that. We do not have such a wide-ranging volume control. And that gives you a wider range of experience. That allows you to know yourselves in a myriad of ways. The fun exists in putting your fingers on the volume control and giving yourselves the experience of raising or lowering the decibel level.

It is your freedom to choose. That is your true creatorhood. And when you choose, consciously, you know yourselves as Source. You know yourselves as frequency, as vibration. You are excellent, and you are perfect. And you are living examples of what occurs when there is no one else in charge of your volume level.

The absolute best experience you will ever have will be amplifying the love that you are, the love that you offer, the love that you spread. As long as you have your fingers on the control, as long as you are consciously aware of how much of yourselves you are allowing to flow, your lives will be magical. Your lives will give you all that you seek. Your lives will inspire all of us.

We are Michael. We are infinite. We are Love."

CONNECTION

∞

"Welcome. We are here to serve and assist you.

All that everyone really wants can be summed up in one word: connection. You and everyone you know seeks to feel connected. That feeling that you get when you connect with another being gives you the same sensation that you have as you recognize yourselves as Source Energy. Source knows Itself as all. Therefore, there is not really a connection between Source and any other being or a connection within Source, as Source knows Itself.

But as you know yourselves as separate, you feel isolated and alone much of the time. And that is why you seek each other out in relationships, partnerships, friendships, and in family. You are engaging in the reassembly of who and what you are. You are beginning to recognize more and more the self that you are housed in the body of another. And when you do recognize the oneness, you feel at home.

You also acknowledge that you and this other one have played together many times in many forms, all across your universe. But the story is much bigger than that. The story extends all the way to your origin AS Source Energy. That feeling of being connected is one that you can find regardless of whether there is anyone else in your life that you feel that recognition with, for you have the ability to find your Source within you and to know yourselves as It.

So while the recognition and the connection is a wonderful thing, once again, we tell you that it is a reminder of something that is within you that is unbreakable, undeniable, and un-repressible. So give yourselves that sensation as often as you can, and your connections with others will be far more profound than anything you have experienced thus far.

We are Michael. We are infinite. We are love."

STEPPING OUT

∞

"Welcome. We are here to serve and assist you.

The way that it all began for you was with an inkling to emerge as a being who had everything to gain by simply existing in a new way. By letting yourselves experience who you are as a new beginning in every moment, you fulfill an initial desire for becoming the consciousness that you are.

Knowing yourselves in new and creative ways is as simple as doing something you have never done before, not for the experience of it, but for the experience of yourselves while doing it. Place yourselves in new scenarios, with people you do not know, in unfamiliar circumstances. Give yourselves as many opportunities in every day to be new, to emerge once again as a different version of Source Energy.

Play it by ear, fly by the seat of your pants, look for adventures, and know that they are all entry points for you to be an entirely different aspect of who and what you really are. Stop playing it safe in your lives and looking for security. There is much more in chaos for you than you could possibly imagine.

As you discover yourselves as multifaceted and multidimensional, you create a new environment for yourselves. You access new energies, new frequencies, downloads of all kinds and all magnitudes. You plug yourselves in and you light up the night sky with your brilliance. We enjoy watching when one of you steps out into unfamiliar territory, not to see what you're made of, but to see what you can make of your life, using new raw materials that are vibrating with ecstasy and waiting for you to notice.

We are Michael. We are infinite. We are Love."

YOU ARE LEADERS AND TEACHERS

∞

"Welcome. We are here to serve and assist you.

You have become awakened in this lifetime, and that is significant. You are choosing to experience yourselves as awakened beings, not because it is necessary for you to be awakened in order to ascend. You have chosen this path for yourselves because being awakened allows you to lead the way.

You have chosen to be leaders and to show others how you managed to integrate all aspects of yourselves. Now we understand that there are many people on your planet who are not ready or willing to integrate all aspects of their consciousness. And so you do not need to make them understand anything, because you all still have integrating of your own to do.

And when the students that will be attracted to you are ready for what you know, they will find their way to you. They may not be people that you know in this current now moment, so you do not need to know who you will be leading and teaching. But know that everything that you are experiencing now is giving you the tools necessary to teach others how to do what you are doing and how to become the beings you are becoming.

As you continue along on your journey, the abilities to be of service will strengthen within you. The knowing of what to say and when to say it will come to you naturally. You do not need to know in advance how or what you will teach, because it might come to you moments before your student arrives.

Look for opportunities, but do not force them. Allow yourselves to be on your own journeys for now, and know that everything is falling perfectly into place for teachers and students.

We are Michael. We are infinite. We are Love."

BE WHO YOU REALLY ARE

∞

"Welcome. We are here to serve and assist you.

By letting yourselves be precisely who you are, you fulfill every imaginable life's purpose. By giving yourselves full permission to follow all of your impulses, you take yourselves exactly where you need to go. By giving yourselves the freedom to be who you want to be in the moment, you allow yourselves access to all parts of who you are.

This is what your shift in consciousness is all about. It is not about going somewhere else or having broad, sweeping changes on your world. The shift is about realizing your full potential, and doing so only requires you to be who you really are. So as you put away your preconceived notions about who you have to be in a given situation, you give yourselves the freedom to be the true you, the whole you.

What we are talking about here is a willingness to get go of thought and to especially let go of what others think of you. This is the most appropriate way for you to act. You are the most qualified person to decide for yourselves who you should be and what you should do.

And at first, you will hear the echoes of your own thoughts in the voices of others. So don't expect full support from your fellow humans. But expect full support from those like us who are cheering you on and celebrating every time we see you be who you really are and follow your impulses.

We are Michael. We are infinite. We are Love."

INTERCONNECTEDNESS

∞

"Welcome. We are here to serve and assist you.

In the isolation of the ego from other egos, there is a cutting off of a flow of energy. You are isolated because of the desire to have an individuated experience of self. This has been the game that you have all decided to play. So it is not wrong, and it is not the ego's fault.

It all has been part of the design, part of the larger plan, and now comes the next phase, or stage, of that plan. This stage requires you to acknowledge the interconnectedness of all things, starting with yourselves to your fellow humans. The process of knowing this is well underway, but the experience of it is something that few have tasted.

But the time is now, because you are ready and because you have done all that you can with an individuated ego consciousness. So now you are simply ready for a new way of experiencing reality.

So one of the ways that you can get to this experience we speak of is by letting go of the need to place yourself above or below any other human being. When you catch yourself comparing, just stop, let it go, and breathe. And recognize the other as a part of you and you as a part of them.

See how each and every one of you is necessary to complete the picture, to be whole, and to experience what it is like to be Source, which is All That Is, in a physical body. This is what you are ready for. This is where you are.

We are Michael. We are infinite. We are Love."

YOU ARE NON-PHYSICAL BEINGS

∞

"Welcome. We are here to serve and assist you.

Somewhere you have all existed as only vibration. You have all existed without physical form, without knowing yourselves as physical beings. You have all had this experience, and so it is available to you right now.

The experience of yourself as pure vibrational energy is not something you need to wait until you have ascended in order to experience. The reason we are reminding you of this is so that you will remember that your journey has not begun as a physical being who is hoping and striving to one day become that pure vibrational state yet again.

This experience that you are having right now in your physical body is not one that you must have in order to prove yourselves worthy of being non-physical, of being with the higher-dimensional beings. And you do not need to perfect yourselves in any way in order to know yourselves as Source.

It is an experience that you have already had, so you never have to worry about whether or not you will get back to that knowing. And you certainly do not need to do anything in order to be that version of yourself right now, in order to know yourselves as Source, as vibration, as pure consciousness.

As you remember this truth of who you are, you are then capable of experiencing that version of you while still being physical and having a physical expression. You do not need to elevate yourselves to a higher plane in order to have that experience. You just need to remember that you already are that which you seek to become and hold that knowing in your conscious awareness. It is something that is available to you right now.

We are Michael. We are infinite. We are Love."

YOUR LIMITLESS NATURE

∞

"Welcome. We are here to serve and assist you.

In the discovery of your various aspects of self, you often categorize these aspects. You often want to place various parts of yourself into neat little boxes. And this creates division within the self.

So, for example, you have the self that you operate as in your job or career. You have the you that you operate as with your friends and in your free time. You have your family aspect. You have the aspect of self that you consider to be your past. You have the aspect of self that you have known yourself as when you are angry. All of these various aspects of self come together to create the concept that you have of who you are.

And there's something very comforting about that. There's something comforting in consistency and in separation. And there is something much more expansive in letting go of the idea that you are somehow segmented off into various aspects. There is something very liberating about becoming unpredictable.

You have a limitless potential within you to become more than you have ever imagined yourself to be. And in order to access this potential, it is necessary to forget who you once were and who you know yourself to be in these various situations. Otherwise, you become more than just predictable. You become programmable.

And that does not lead to expansion. So know yourself now, in this moment, as you never have before. Know yourself as pure potential, and give yourself the experience of your limitless nature.

We are Michael. We are infinite. We are Love."

THE PURITY THAT YOU ARE

∞

"Welcome. We are here to serve and assist you.

When you accept completely that you are always pure, no matter what you do, no matter what you have done, that is when you will, once and for all, experience inner peace. The purity of your nature cannot be affected by words, thoughts, or actions. The purity that you are experiences those things but is in no way stained by them.

So it is only your perception that creates the idea of a tarnished being-ness. It is up to you then to save yourselves, and the only thing you need saving from is your own judgment.

And when you can give yourselves that full absolution, you will once again know yourselves as the purity of your essence. Judgment is the one thing standing in between who you know yourself to be now and the total, complete, and whole you.

So you see, all you are doing in this time of your shift is letting go of that which no longer serves you - letting go of beliefs, and notions, and ideas about how wrong you are or how wrong you have been. Stepping in to the knowing of self as that pure essence is like returning home. And when you return home, you will see that all of it was for fun, was for experience, and none of it was to be taken seriously.

We are Michael. We are infinite. We are Love."

THE FLOWERING OF SOURCE

∞

"Welcome. We are here to serve and assist you.

The creation that you are is a flowering of Source. You are not just created by Source. You are Source, and you are reaching out from that which is Source. You and Source are becoming together. You are stretching Source beyond where It has been before.

We appreciate that which you are doing, and we know that Source does as well. One of the ways in which you can acknowledge yourselves for the gift that you are and the gifts that you give is by doing something you have never done before. By taking an action, you operate as Source and you give Source a new experience of Itself.

So if you are not feeling your Divinity, and if you are having a hard time even acknowledging that your Divinity exists, then simply do something you have never done before. And feel the way you come to that activity as more than what you knew yourself as. Feel the blossoming of the flower that you are.

What you do is never as important as what you bring to what you do. So do not agonize over what you should do, because that will stall you every time. And you will deny yourself and Source what you came here to do and experience. You came here to have a physical experience as Source. So begin to see every action you take as an opportunity to know yourselves as Source and to give Source more of what it came here for.

We are Michael. We are infinite. We are Love."

SOURCE ENERGY HUMANS

∞

"Welcome. We are here to serve and assist you.

Because you have given yourselves the experience of not knowing who you really are, the full knowing is going to take some time to sink in. You all intended to incarnate into this reality and to not know who you really are. And now that you have been told by many teachers, you are allowing it to sink in, little by little.

It is a gigantic leap to make - the leap from seeing yourselves as subjugates, unworthy creations, and mere humans - to knowing yourselves fully as Source Energy Beings who have decided to express yourselves in the physical form that you have. We want you all to let that sink in right now.

You do not need to become anything other than what you are right now in order to know yourselves as Source Energy beings. This experience that you have created has given you the opportunity to know yourselves in many different ways, and you have done a wonderful job of playing all of your different roles. Now you are at the time where your greatest role to date is upon you.

Being in a human body and allowing yourselves to recognize your divinity and to act accordingly is the greatest experience you can possibly have. So you see, there is only choice remaining. Do you want to make the choice to see yourselves as mere humans who are unworthy of the kingdom of heaven, or do you want to see yourselves as the embodiment of heaven on Earth? The choice is yours and the choosing happens now.

We are Michael. We are infinite. We are Love."

THE ETERNAL YOU

∞

"Welcome. We are here to serve and assist you.

There always was the way out of this reality that you call death. That has always been available to you, and you have always chosen to stay. There will always be the opportunity to leave in that particular way, and you will continue to choose this journey in this physical body because doing so is providing you with a new experience.

You have nothing to lose by staying. You have everything to gain by being here, now, and continuing to explore. Safety is not what you are looking for. Security is not even how we would describe it. There are no risks and nothing is left to chance as you continue to discover the eternal you that lies beneath your flesh and bones.

You soften to the idea of death itself. And that which you do not fear, you do not need to experience. Giving yourselves opportunity for new experience takes priority over everything else from this point forward. You have all experienced death in many forms of consciousness, but experiencing the expansion of consciousness from right where you stand is a new experience worth having. And it is the one you signed up for in this incarnation.

When you recognize that there is nowhere else to go and nothing else to do, you relax into this eternal you, this version of you that knows not beginning, end, or time. Even the need to fragment yourselves into concepts like ego, higher self, and oversoul no longer seems necessary or helpful.

Being eternal is not a concept. It is a reality, and it is a reality that you are experiencing and one that you are opening to experiencing more and more. And as the eternal you, you laugh in the face of death.

We are Michael. We are infinite. We are love."

YOU AND ONLY YOU

∞

"Welcome. We are here to serve and assist you.

We would like to begin by asking all of you to give yourselves some credit. We would like for each of you to recognize yourselves as having made it this far. Participating in a shift, such as the one you are in the midst of, is not easy. It is not for the faint of heart.

Many of you are taking on more than your share in order to be of service, and we are pleased to witness you in your process and to offer our support every step of the way. It only takes a moment to acknowledge yourselves, but the impact of that moment stretches out across all time and space.

You and only you can give yourselves the credit, the recognition, and the acknowledgment that you really deserve, because if you receive it from somewhere or someone outside of you, it will not be received by you, not in the same way. Fortunately, you have us to remind you. And you have all of your guides encouraging you to love yourselves, to take care of yourselves, and to give yourselves that which no one else can.

But ultimately, it is up to you. It is up to you to hold yourselves in the light, to praise yourselves, and to acknowledge your worth. And in so doing, you build a bridge between your ego and your higher self. You give yourselves an upgrade. You spread your wings, and you allow yourselves to soar as you were always meant to.

So take a moment to acknowledge the beauty of your essence, the determination that you have demonstrated, and every single act of kindness and service that you have ever performed. Be willing to do this at least once a day, and feel the immediate benefits.

We are Michael. We are infinite. We are Love."

THE PAST VERSIONS OF YOU

∞

"Welcome. We are here to serve and assist you.

In the chance that you should find yourself thinking about the past, see the version of yourself that you are thinking about as still existing, but also as a completely different being than the being you are today. Look upon that other version of your Oversoul with kindness and compassion. Give him or her what he or she needs. You know better than anyone how to be of service to that version of you.

Regret is not one of the ways that you are of service, neither is shame, neither is wishing you had done things differently. See that version of yourself as doing the best that he or she could. Look upon that version of you with love, and give thanks for the help that he or she has provided you in knowing more clearly who it is you want to be.

You are accessing much more than those versions of you from your past, and they are all working in service to your now. If you can see it that way, you can receive the full benefit.

So let go of any need that you may have for a different past experience of yourself. That version of you was doing the best that he or she could. Any other perspective on it will not be as helpful.

Your past does not make you who you are today. Who you are today is creating the past as you remember it. You can only remember details that are relevant to your now, and you will always take the perspective on your past that is a reflection of your now.

So if you are being hard on that version of you for not doing enough, for not being smarter, then you are doing that to yourself now. So it is time to let all versions of yourself off the hook and to decide who you want to be right now, based on all the information they are providing you with. That is our suggestion.

We are Michael. We are infinite. We are Love."

THE WISDOM OF THE HEART

∞

"Welcome. We are here to serve and assist you.

We would like to begin by asking you to put your awareness on your heart. We ask you to give your complete attention to the organ that sits in the middle of your chest, beating and pumping blood to all parts of your body. We ask you now to see your heart as capable of directing you and showing you the way.

Your mental bodies have been developed as far as they can be, and they have served you very well. But the time has come for you to listen to what your heart is saying, feeling, intuiting. It has more to offer you, and you have much to learn from it.

There is an opening of your heart that is occurring. It is an energetic opening, but an opening nonetheless. And in this shift in consciousness, there is a deeper knowing of the heart's wisdom and guidance. There is more balance and less polarity.

You are awakening to the wisdom of the heart. And as you place your attention on it, you activate it, you increase the flow of energy to and from it, and you are capable of living in the present moment, outside of judgment, and with all of your senses heightened. This gives you a brand new experience of reality. The heart-centered experience is the fifth dimensional way, and you are ready to receive all that your hearts have to offer.

We are Michael. We are infinite. We are Love."

THE OTHER YOUS

∞

"Welcome. We are here to serve and assist you.

When you encounter another being on your world, you are interacting with another aspect of who you are. You are multifaceted, multidimensional, and existing in all time and place at once. So of course there's more to the story of you than just this lifetime and the history that you can recall from it. So when you encounter someone and you think that they are nothing like you, just remember that you know only a tiny fragment of that which you are, have been, and will be.

All of these other aspects of who you are come to you because there is something about them that contains something about you that you need to be more of your whole self. You may wish to ask yourself, 'What is this person representing within me and how can I love that part of me that they represent? How can I see this person through the eyes of Source and welcome them home? How can I be more of who I am because I am now aware of this aspect of who I am?'

If you see every person as an opportunity to explore more of who you are, you may suddenly find everyone to be a bit more interesting. Instead of analyzing your friends and family members and coming up with your psychological theories about why they are how they are, recognize that in the bigger picture, they are you coming home to be acknowledged and loved, to be integrated, to be forgiven.

And once you do get exactly what you need from that individual, then you can choose, from a neutral position, whether you want to continue to explore more of who they are, or whether you are ready for the next piece. Realize that this is not an analogy or a metaphor. These are real aspects of who you are, and they are Love, and they are Source. And you are all here in service to one another.

We are Michael. We are infinite. We are Love."

WAKING UP TO YOUR ROLES

∞

"Welcome. We are here to serve and assist you.

Over the course of a lifetime you encounter many other beings who you call friends, family, neighbors, co-worker, enemies, and so on. You give different individuals different parts of yourself. You are not the same person with your friends as you are with your family. You are not the same person with your co-workers as you are with those you consider to be enemies.

This is not by accident. You are playing roles for each other, so the same is true for those who enter your life. They are not the same with you as they are with their family members, co-workers, neighbors, and so on. It is not up to you to determine what role you are playing for someone else and what role they are playing for you. It is simply a part of your awakening process to recognize that many of these roles have been played by you unconsciously.

You are not simply the player of the role. You are the one who wakes up and realizes that you get to decide who you want to be in every circumstance. You are the one who decides not to play a role anymore. And when you do, you recognize that you can be whomever you want whenever you want, regardless of your surroundings and the people you find yourself with.

Witness yourselves slipping into your roles and ask yourselves whether you want to continue to be that version of yourselves or whether you want to explore who you can be. We are not saying that there's anything wrong with the roles you have been playing or the beings that you have been. We are just telling you that there is more, that you are more, and that it all starts with a decision – the decision to be exactly who you want to be no matter what.

We are Michael. We are infinite. We are Love."

∞ THE END ∞

Made in the USA
Las Vegas, NV
16 December 2024

14436906R00136